Living Light as a Feather

How to Find Joy in Every Day and a Purpose in Every Problem

Ruth Fishel

Health Communications, Inc.
Deerfield Beach, Florida

www.hci-online.com

Prayers for Sophia. Excerpted from *Prayers for Sophia* by Joyce Rupp. ©2004 by Joyce Rupp, published by Ave Maria Press, P.O. Box 428, Notre Dame, Indiana 46556. Used with permission of the publisher. *www.avemariapress.com.*

Merger poem ©1979 by Judy Chicago. Used with permission.

Library of Congress Cataloging-in-Publication Data is available from the Library of Congress.

ISBN 0-7573-0157-6

Publisher: Health Communications, Inc.
          3201 S.W. 15th Street
          Deerfield Beach, FL 33442–8190

Cover photo ©Getty Images, Inc.
Cover and inside book design by Lawna Patterson Oldfield

LIVING LIGHT AS A FEATHER

I dedicate this book to

the day when all hearts can feel joy,

when our sole purpose is to spread love

and when war is but a

distant memory.

Contents

Preface

Dear Readers,

How can we even consider living light as a feather when so much heaviness is filling our world? Wouldn't that mean that we are taking life too lightly? With terrorism, wars, poverty and abuse, just to name a few of the horrors that fill our daily headlines, isn't it more appropriate to be angry, seek revenge and force change via war?

The truth is we have no choice. Anger and revenge perpetuate violence and war, and we will continue to be in pain. We must find a new direction for peace and there is only one place to find it. That is to look inside. When I find it in me, it can fill my world, and its energy can spread out to others. When each of us finds our own path to peace, our energy can spread farther and farther until it touches the hearts of everyone.

A few years ago my publisher, Peter Vegso, fascinated me with stories of Egyptian mythology. One myth, called "Weighing the Heart," struck me particularly. It illustrated that when a person dies his or her heart is placed on one side of a scale and a feather is placed on the other side. If his or her heart is as light as a feather, the person's soul would live forever in eternity. When I heard this, something happened in my heart, and I felt a great softening around it. I was totally one with the moment, barely breathing. I felt as if my heart sighed. Instantly, creative inspiration poured through me, and I knew that here was my next book. I saw it clearly laid out before me like a beautifully wrapped gift.

The table of contents was all outlined in an instant in my mind. My soul expanded because I knew I had received a very special invitation. I was to write *Living Light as a Feather*, and gratefully, excitedly, enthusiastically, I accepted the task with a mental bow.

I humbly offer the results of that wonderful moment to you, my reader. May it unlock anything that has been hiding in your heart that is a barrier to your peace and joy. May it guide you on your journey to purpose and offer support as you expand your spiritual path.

Living Light as a Feather offers practical, clear steps to letting go of obstacles and showing how to replace them with powerful, spiritual qualities that lighten hearts and inspire joy. You will learn the Heart-Lightening Process, simple steps that can take you from a place of pain or uncertainty to a place of joy and purpose.

May your life be a story of abundance, joy, love and peace.

Live lightly!

With love and peace,
Ruth Fishel
Marstons Mills, Cape Cod, MA
March 11, 2004

Acknowledgments

I am so deeply grateful to Sandy Bierig, who has edited all my books before they go to the publisher. Sandy has worked especially hard at this one, editing all the stories of the people whom I interviewed. Sandy thought she retired a few years ago. Little did she know how busy she would be!

An enormous thanks to Allison Janse, my editor at Health Communications, Inc., for all her patience, terrific suggestions, thought-provoking questions and her final editing. It has been a joy working with you!

Nancy Burke, your input has been a great addition to this book, and I am so very appreciative.

Thank you, artist Lawna Oldfield, for doing such a wonderful job with the cover and inside design.

Many thanks go to my daughters, Debbie Boisseau and Judy Fishel, and friends Sharon Anderson, Pat DeSciscio, Joan Driscoll, Elaine Emery, Joan Graham, Mimi Kahn, Kate McCarthy-Martin, Gina Ogden, Carol Plummer, Kathy Roach, Barbara Thomas, Gina Tonelli, Maggie Salvitori and Nancy Wellington for their helpful feedback and encouragement.

I have such a warm place in my heart for Anne and Paul for their generous gift of my home away from home, a beautiful, quiet and inspiring space where I could get away, stare at the ocean and birds, think and write.

I am so grateful for the many people who have participated in this book. I'll not mention names here, as many of you wish to remain anonymous, but you know who you are. I want to thank those of you who shared your stories with me that, for some reason or other, did not get into the book, either because the story was similar to another one or just from lack of space.

I'm grateful to Chas DiCapua at IMS and Joanne Friday for clearing up my questions on Buddhist philosophy.

A enormous thanks to all my teachers Sylvia Boorstein, Christina Feldman, Joseph Goldstein, Jack Kornfield, Narayan Liebenson Grady, Larry Rosenberg and Sharon Salzman; and my special friends, authors and workshop leaders who have taught me so much.

And a big thanks to publisher Peter Vegso, for his confidence in my ability to write this book and thus continue to help people find their joy and purpose.

To Dr. Bob and Bill Wilson. Without them I would not be here today.

CHAPTER

1

Living Lightly

The Secret

The Creator gathered all of Creation and said,
"I want to hide something from the humans
until they are ready for it.
It is the realization that
they create their own reality."
The eagle said, "Give it to me, I will take it to the moon."
The Creator said, "No. One day they will go there and find it."
The salmon said, "I will bury it on the bottom of the ocean."
"No. They will go there, too."
The buffalo said, "I will bury it on the Great Plains."
The Creator said, "They will cut into the skin of the Earth
and find it even there."
Grandmother Mole, who lives in the breast of Mother Earth,
and who has no physical eyes but sees with spiritual eyes,
said, "Put it inside of them."
And the Creator said, "It is done."

—A Sioux Myth

Weeping may linger for the night, but
joy comes with the morning.

—Psalms 30:5

There is an ancient Chinese tale about a woman whose only son died. In her grief, she went to the holy man and said, "What prayers, what magical incantations can you do to bring my son back to life?"

Instead of sending her away, he said to her, "Fetch me a mustard seed from a home that has never known sorrow. We will use it to drive the sorrow out of your life."

The woman went off at once in search of that magical mustard seed. She came first to a splendid mansion, knocked at the door and said, "I am looking for a home that has never known sorrow. Is this such a place?"

"You've certainly come to the wrong place," they said, and began to describe the myriad of tragic things that had befallen them. The woman said to herself, "Who is better able to help these poor, unfortunate people than I, who have had misfortune of my own?"

She stayed to comfort them, then went on in search of a home that had never known sorrow. But wherever she turned, at farmhouses, inns and the city, she found one tale after another of sadness and misfortune. She became so involved in ministering to other people's grief that ultimately she forgot about her quest for the magical mustard seed, never realizing that the search had, in fact, driven the sorrow out of her life.

All of us suffer. Perhaps our parents weren't emotionally available to us as much as we needed, or the neighborhood kids called us names. Childhood incidents that seemed trivial can leave a lasting impression, contributing to our suffering years later, even when we are not aware of them. Or perhaps you've suffered a job loss after working for the same company for thirty years or have been diagnosed with a life-threatening illness. Perhaps you struggle with an addiction or are feeling the pain when someone dear to your heart has died. Everyone struggles with suffering and pain, and none of us can avoid disappointments and discontent.

The degree of our suffering is personal and cannot be compared to that of others. Nor do we all heal in the same way or according to any predetermined timetable. Some of us move on after experiencing a tragedy, becoming stronger and finding a new or deeper purpose in our lives. Others never completely heal but somehow learn to live with the pain. And, sadly, some become stuck, unable to move on.

How we respond to our experiences is also determined individually. Whether we block them, deny them, hold on to them or accept them and let them take their natural course are choices that are within our power to make.

As the Sioux myth at the beginning of the chapter explains, we create our own reality. Therefore, if our intention is to live a life of joy and purpose, and if our thoughts are focused on this intention, then this is the direction our lives take. We might have to overcome many obstacles. We might have to uncover many layers of memories, but we can eventually find joy and purpose.

But how do you find joy when you're in the midst of pain? You don't, at first! It is important to know that finding joy in every day is a goal, an intention, and may not always be possible.

Discovering how to live as light as a feather is easier than we think, but we must be willing to go through the process of letting go of whatever is necessary in order to arrive at that lighter place in life. We have to let go of preconceived ideas, judgments, resentments and much more. Each time we uncover another layer, our hearts become lighter. Each time we become willing to let go of another block or another burden, our hearts become lighter. And in this space, which was once filled by darkness, light now shines, and love and compassion can take their rightful places and fill our hearts with joy.

We have to go to the very center of our being to get to know who we really are. This book will help you do this with a seven-step Heart-Lightening Process.

Soul Searching

The idea for this book was inspired by an Egyptian myth that explains what happens to a person's soul after death. The deceased is ushered to the Hall of Double Justice and stands before Osiris, the Good One, who performs a judgment. A vast scale sits in the center of the room where Maat, Goddess of truth, justice and balance stands ready to begin the afterlife ceremonial weighing of the deceased's heart. A feather, the symbol of truth, is placed in a container on one side of the scale and the heart, or conscience, of the deceased is placed on the other side. If the two sides of the scale are in perfect balance, Osiris renders a favorable judgment: "Let the deceased depart victorious. Let him go wherever he wishes, to mingle freely with the gods. He is worthy of joining the gods in the fields of peace." The deceased, thus justified, goes on to live a life of eternal happiness.[1]

The first time I heard this myth I felt tingles going up and down my spine and goose pimples on my arms. If our hearts are as light as a feather, our soul lives on forever! I knew there was a book in this story and I began exploring questions such as, "What do we have to do to make our hearts as light as a feather while we are alive?"

Defining the soul is a very personal matter; therefore, how you interpret it is up to you. I don't think anyone "knows." Albert Schweitzer once said that we couldn't fully define "soul" because to define anything is to set the limits of our own minds around it. But we can sense the soul—something that is higher than our individual self, yet is the essence of our self. The soul is our aspiration for truth, beauty and the desire to do good. It reminds me of what Eric Fromm wrote about defining God. He said that man is finite. God is infinite. Therefore, man can never truly know God. Many people state with authority that they "know" what the soul is—and all these definitions vary. Each "expert" who knows for sure differs from the next "expert" who knows for sure.

To me, soul is really an idea, a concept, a word we use to define the indefinable, the unseen. Soul is nonmaterial and metaphysical. It is the very essence or spirit of our life. It connects us with our hearts, with our feelings of love, truth and joy. It holds our purpose.

In their series Mysteries of the Unknown, the editors of Time-Life Books published *Search for the Soul*,[2] and included a fascinating story about James Kidd, a seventy-year-old Arizona miner and prospector who had disappeared and was assumed dead. He was known to be shabby and frugal and had a "quirky way of sky gazing that marked him as something of a benign eccentric." He would frequently scramble onto the tin roof of the miner's pump house to gaze upward and study the stars. He stared at the sky "as if transported into a distant world." Kidd lived simply and he left behind a fortune consisting of stocks and dividends worth over $174,000.

The story fascinated Geraldine Swift, an Arizona estate tax commissioner, who found that Kidd had no living relatives. Still, she resisted the pressure to have the state be the recipient of his fortune. Fifteen years after Kidd disappeared, she found a scrap of lined notebook paper in his records, which turned out to be a will. He asked that his money go into research for "some scientific proof of a soul of the human body, which leaves at death." Kidd wanted confirmation of the existence of the human soul.

The researchers of the Parapsychology Foundation spent $275,455 but could find nothing conclusive. Their report was duly chronicled by the *New York Times* in its June 16, 1975, issue under the headline, "Researchers Aided by Hermit's Will Fail to Find a Soul."

Kidd had hoped that the results of this research would produce a photograph of an actual soul. But instead, the research proved what we all know: The soul can't be seen, touched, smelled, heard or tasted. It is known only by our intuition, our inner know-ing, our faith.

Transforming Our Pain into Our Purpose

Problems are only opportunities
in work clothes.

—Henry J. Kaiser

Many times we see something as a problem when it really isn't one at all. What we are going through or what is happening is a fact, a situation that we simply have to accept. A problem is a set of circumstances that threatens our well-being. Circumstances are people, places or things. We can't change people, places or things. We can only change ourselves. For example, you might have lost most of your retirement money in the stock market. Now you think you can't retire. That is not a problem. That is a fact. If we look at this and accept it as a fact and not a problem, then we can say, "What can I do about it?" If we look at this as a problem, we stay stuck.

The Buddhist monk, teacher and writer, Thich Nhat Hanh, writes that "The extinction of one thing brings about the birth of something else. When darkness is extinguished, light comes forth. When suffering is removed, peace and happiness are always there." It is said that pain is the touchstone of all spiritual growth. When you find yourself in the midst of a painful situation, very often a new purpose appears.

I believe that one of the reasons that we are on this planet is to find our purpose, which changes as we change. Once we find it, we know what to do with our lives in each moment. I believe we must make a connection with God or a power greater than ourselves in order to do this, because our soul is our connection to God, and our purpose lies in our soul. There's a wonderful story that reveals how God broke the biggest star into millions and millions of pieces. Then God placed one piece into each person's heart. And that is how we received our souls. Therefore, once we can uncover, discover and connect with our souls, our spirits, the true essence of who we are, we can find our connection to God and the universe.

I believe we all have a purpose. Some of us find it early in life, without any struggle. Those of us who paint, write or have a natural skill for music, or who absolutely know they want to be a veterinarian or teacher or the best parent they can be, are fortunate. Many of us struggle to find what it is that fulfills us. Some of us never find it. And many find it through pain and loss. Poet David Whyte says that "through the rawness of our wounds we touch the world." Many of the stories you will read in this book recount profound personal tragedies that ultimately lead to a turning point in someone's life, where someone's unfilled need becomes obvious and they jump into the void to fill it.

Author Dr. John F. Demartin writes, "Wisdom is the instantaneous recognition that a crisis is a blessing, and even greater wisdom recognizes that blessings can also trigger a crisis. When we truly understand that, we're less likely to be upset about difficulties or elated about opportunities; we remain centered no matter what happens around us. That is one of the secrets of self-mastery."

How many times have you asked: What is the purpose of my life? Why am I here? What do I want to do with my life? Who am I?

Rabbi David Cooper, in his wonderful book *God Is a Verb,* writes, "Once we fully appreciate that our purpose is not to achieve some transcendental level but to deal with the imperfect world as a partner in creation, we gain the very thing we turn away from. That is to say when we surrender to the fact that we will constantly be repairing our own souls and those of others around us, we gain a new sense of the fullness of each moment. When we accept each moment as an opportunity for fulfilling our purpose, we are always present, always succeeding, always changing the world for the better."[3]

Is it all part of a divine plan? It seems to flow that way. We hear stories all the time about how one person's tragedy was the motivation to help others, making life a little better for all of us. This is not to say that God lets bad things happen so that people can be helped. I do not believe that God moves people around, as if on a chessboard. I agree with Rabbi Harold Kushner who writes that tragedy happens at random and randomness is another name for chaos. He tells us that the laws of nature do not make exceptions for nice people. "All we can do is rise beyond the question, 'Why did this happen?' and begin to ask the question 'What do I do now that this has happened?'"[4] Thich Nhat Hanh writes that it is our responsibility as human beings to let our suffering transform the suffering of those around us. We need not worry about finding someone we can help. We simply need to open our eyes and our hearts. And as Mother Teresa showed us by example, "You love one leper at a time. You love the one in front of you."

Maybe you think you are here on Earth for one particular reason, only to be surprised to find that something else is stirring below the level of consciousness. Once you have stopped long enough, it has the opportunity to surface and present itself to you.

Sandy Bierig, who cofounded, with me, Serenity House—a halfway house program for alcoholic women—put it this way: "It was as if everything I had ever experienced or believed told me exactly how to create the program. When I was given a grant to found the sobriety program at the Massachusetts Correctional Institute for Women, I had never been in prison except for a crazy tour when I followed the women's caucus of the state legislature while they were on a fact-finding trip. I just *knew* what to do about the in-house program I designed. I knew how to talk to the inmates, the guards and the administrators, and I knew what my goals should be. I was never afraid and saw people only as human beings who were on a different path."

Our purpose does not have to change the world, as Candy Lightner aimed to do. Lightner founded MADD (Mothers Against Drunk Driving) after she lost her young daughter to a senseless and entirely preventable accident caused by a drunk driver. She transformed her rage into a campaign to raise awareness of the havoc drunk drivers create, to see that they were punished for the death and destruction they caused and, perhaps wishfully, to rid the United States of drunk drivers entirely.

Our purpose may not become as widely known, but it can be as equally important in the scheme of the world. Lois and Julielyn are wonderful examples of this.

~

Lois' bright and beautiful and brave oldest daughter, Julielyn, was diagnosed with Crohn's disease at the age of fifteen. It is a very serious illness and was totally unexpected. There is no known cause or cure for the disease, and people don't like to talk about it because it involves the colon and body wastes and can only be relieved by drastic surgery. Lois has experienced moments of great sadness and fear because Julie has had to undergo seventy hospitalizations and thirty-four surgeries.

Any parent wants so badly for his or her child to go to school and succeed there. Lois said, "Our Julie desperately wanted to finish just one semester when she didn't get an incomplete for her work because she spent so much time out of class. Near death so many times, she doesn't let herself fall into self-pity. She has found a way to transform her pain into action steps to help other sufferers and their families change their attitudes and find hope."

Julie explains, "You have to take the ugliness out of the disease and find the beauty in it. The beauty is in the support of so many wonderful people who help one to learn to relish the moment."

Lois, too, is open to the moment. "I know totally that Julie is in good hands with her doctors. I've learned when to stick my neck out and when to let go and let God. I don't dwell on the fact that she could be gone tomorrow. I embrace the goodness that comes out of my pain and find the harmony that God has given to me in a very deep place." Julie, too, gets through each challenge by strengthening her relationship with God through prayer and meditation.

Because hers is a progressive form of the illness, Julie and her family feel they have no time for pettiness, and they try hard to achieve balance in their lives. One year, when Julie was serving as a counselor at summer camp for people like herself, she called her mother on her twenty-first birthday to say she was having so much fun at the camp with the kids. "Mom, this is the best week of my life. I feel so normal."

Today, Julie is a motivational speaker for those affected by Crohn's disease. She remains a counselor at the Ostomy Camp for Children, and she has created a Web page called Life With Fred *through which she communicates with people all over the world. Asked what she has learned from her experience with her daughter's illness, Lois says, "I have learned the necessity of balance in life for myself and others and about what it really means to rise above negativity and crises. I have learned that God is everywhere and will never, never let the sun set without bringing another sunrise. I understand the true necessity for God in all things and in every circumstance. This alignment then carries me like a well-made bridge into a closeness with him every day. My daughter's losses create a greater hunger for God in me. God has more clearly defined my purpose and opened so many avenues to see him and serve him in all things. My strength and kindness are increased, and I am humbled daily because of the path I have traveled. This path has given friends, family, strangers and myself chances to shine and*

grow in ways that otherwise might have been unknown. I have
been blessed with relationships and resources previously
untapped and have learned to thank God in all circum-
stances."

Do you sometimes feel that something inside of you is missing? You can almost see it, but it just keeps slipping away. It's the
secret to life and you're sure that everyone knows what it is but
you. It's what other people seem to know instinctively and about
which you don't have a clue. Somewhere in your heart lies joy and
you can't reach it. It keeps eluding you. You think you have the
answer . . . more money, a better job, the perfect partner. When
you think you do have it, it only lasts for a while, sometimes for
years. Eventually, however, the joy always goes and you find yourself reaching for something, anything, that might bring it back:
bungie jumping, new clothes or another drink. If only we knew
that the key has always been there. We just can't see it. All our
grasping and reaching and wanting and craving blocks our view.

There's a wonderful story about a man who has lost his keys.
He goes out onto the sidewalk, under the street lamp, and looks
and looks and looks. A friend comes along and asks him what he
is doing.

"I'm looking for my keys."

"Did you lose them here?"

"No, but the light is brighter here."

This book will show you how, through a seven-step process,

you can learn to look in the right places to lighten your life and find joy and purpose. Remember the Sioux myth from the beginning of this chapter? God placed the realization that we create our own reality inside of us, just where Grandmother Mole suggested. Once we look within, we will find both the blocks that have been keeping us stuck and the keys to unlocking them.

Some of us have to suffer greatly before we can cry out to some unknown force somewhere out in the deepest darkness of the night. Others are lucky enough to suffer only slightly, and they find the key, their purpose, early in life. A few, the lucky minority, were brought up by a family who already had found their key to life and passed it on through unconditional love, support, encouragement. Not everyone accepts this gift. Some reject it, going out on their own until pain and suffering finally bring them home to the truth.

Once you find your purpose, your life will never be the same. It does not have to be found through religion, although it can be. It is a simple letting go to a power greater than ourselves, an acceptance that we don't rule the universe, that we don't have control over everything in our lives and the lives of others. It is knowing that there is a rhythm and a pattern in the universe and we can tap into it when we allow ourselves to be open. We arrive at a place where we finally know that we cannot come to true joy and purpose and fulfillment alone.

But once we find it, the journey is only beginning. Our hearts are still blocked and we have to remove those blocks. It's a simple journey, clearly laid out by spiritual masters long before us. Our job is to remove the blocks that we carry in our heavy hearts. These blocks have been variously called the seven deadly sins, character defects, flaws and imperfections. Author, scholar and psychologist James Hillman tells us that "you have to give up the life you have to get the life that's waiting for you."

Know that we will never be free of these blocks completely. Our task is to have the intention, the willingness, the openness to let them go. And once we begin this journey, even for a moment, we get an instant vision of the promise of joy. Once we make a beginning to lighten our burden, we discover what fills our hearts with love and joy. And our hearts become lighter and lighter.

Living Light as a Feather offers practical, clear steps for letting go of obstacles and shows you how to replace them with powerful, spiritual qualities that lighten hearts and inspire joy. The Heart-Lightening Process will teach you simple steps that can take you from a place of pain or uncertainty to a place of joy and purpose.

What is burning in your soul right now? Perhaps you have been drawn to this book to uncover your blocks, eliminate your "should's," put aside your "ought to's," get acquainted or reacquainted with your soul, lighten your heart and find your true purpose. I suggest you take a notebook and use it only for this journey. Why not take some time to see where you are right now and really get to know yourself?

Are your beliefs still those of early childhood, what you learned from your parents, rabbi, priest or teacher? Take time to go inside and find your own answers. Take time to find out who you

Feathers

Feathers are wonderful images, which can help us feel lighter. Let your imagination take over and picture a feather. Imagine it floating above you on a very gentle breeze. Watch it as it gently falls into your outstretched hand. Feel its softness as it brushes against the skin of the palm of your hand.

Feathers conjure up so many wonderful images, from flying, to freedom, to nature, to softness, to pillows! Feathers speak to us of flight, of going beyond boundaries, of getting "above it all," or of the need to let go and travel lightly. As far back as ancient Egyptian, Asian and Celtic eras, feathers carried prayers to heavenly gods and bestowed extraordinary powers in battle. They have served as spiritual symbols for healing, prayer and sacred power in cultures that communicated with nature in ways that have been overlooked or forgotten in our own time. They represent the creative force for Native Americans.

Feathers are very fragile and they have to be handled with care, just as we have to learn to handle ourselves with care. You, too, can feel lighter. You can learn to experience your life as light as a feather but it is not something that happens overnight. It is a process that grows because of your willingness to stop and look with new eyes at where you are in the present moment. As Zen Master Dogen said, "We will look with eyes unclouded by longing."[5]

really are. Take time for silence. Take time for nature. Let this book flow for you. Let it soothe you. Above all . . . be gentle with yourself! Ask yourself:

- What does "my true self" mean today?
- When was I the most "free to be me"—if ever?

- When did I feel the greatest joy?
- Can I remember a time when this joy was stifled? Put down? Stopped? Inhibited?
- What are my values?
- What do I hold most dear?
- What stirs me . . . moves me emotionally? Spiritually?
- Have I found my life's purpose for now?
- Who most influenced my life in a positive way?
- If I could be in any part of the world for as long as I wanted to, where would I go?
- What would I do?

Now add your own soul-searching questions to this list.

The following chapters will help you explore the questions:

- How do I get from "out there" to "in here"?
- How do I know when to hold on and when to let go?
- What blocks joy from my life?
- Do I have a purpose?
- And if I do, how can I find it?

The Heart-Lightening Process

First a person should put his house together,
then his town, then the world.

—Rabbi Israel Salanter

The Heart-Lightening Process consists of steps we can take to raise our energy to a higher level, find joy in every day and purpose in every problem. The first two steps begin the process. The rest of the steps are what I call "floating steps," and can be used in any order that works best for you. Each situation differs.

The Heart-Lightening Process
Step 1:

STOP AND BE IN THE PRESENT MOMENT

The very first step in learning to live as lightly as a feather is to stop and be in the present moment. Simply take in a deep breath and as you breathe in, feel your breath filling your heart. Be aware of your chest rising and your stomach expanding as your lungs fill with air. Keep your entire attention on your breath, then let it out, and watch your chest and your stomach contract. Notice any awareness you might have of your body, such as warm hands or a feeling of lightness. This very simple technique takes you out of your head and away from the thoughts that create your feelings. As it says in the Bible, "Be still and know that I am God."

Begin by practicing with your breath. It's especially useful when you are feeling fearful, angry, confused, upset or tense. If you are in any of these states, you are not in the present moment. You are in your thoughts and your thoughts take you into the past or the future. For example, if you are angry, you're reliving something that happened in the past. If you're fearful, you're projecting into the future something that hasn't happened yet.

There is a wonderful Zen story that illustrates the value of stopping.

There was a man so displeased by the sight of his own shadow and so displeased with his own footsteps that he determined to be rid of both. The method he hit upon was to run away from them. So he got up and ran. But every time he put his foot down his foot made another shadow, keeping up with him without the slightest difficulty. He attributed his failure to the fact that he was not running fast enough. So he ran faster and faster without stopping, until he finally dropped dead. He failed to realize that if he merely stepped into the shade, his shadow would vanish, and if he sat down and stayed still, there would be no more footsteps.

—Chuang Tzu

Today is a perfect beginning for wherever you are on your spiritual journey. When our attention is in our head with our thoughts, we are not in the present moment. Instead, we are either in the past or in the future. If we feel anything but peace, we are not in the present moment because when we are in the present moment, we are connected to God, our hearts, and souls, and then everything is perfect and we are at peace.

As much as you may argue that you are not perfect, that you don't feel perfect because you don't have this or that in your life, or that you have too much of this or that, or that you aren't the person you would like to be—you really are perfect in this moment. I'm not saying that you are necessarily happy in this moment. Nor am I saying that you are sad in this moment. But you are perfect, and you do have everything you need in this moment.

Wherever you are today is perfect.
You've been arriving right here, right now in this moment in time
*   and space.*
You're here to make a new beginning on your spiritual journey and
*   to experience and accept joy in your life.*
Everything you've done in your entire life has led you to this very
*   moment and it is perfect. Accept yourself just as you are.*
Completely.
Know that you are perfect and let yourself feel the joy of this knowledge.
                                        —*Time for Joy,* Ruth Fishel [6]

Take a moment and imagine you are on a ladder. Each rung of the ladder represents a different level of energy. The rung at the bottom of the ladder is suffering, the lowest energy; at the top is joy, the highest. In between are all the other emotions, negative and positive. You can barely feel any energy on the lower rungs—when you are full of fear, self-doubt, insecurity and jealousy—but as you move up to the emotions of generosity, forgiveness, compassion and love, you feel more power. You feel flooded with joy. Take a moment to see where you are on this ladder.

Practicing Meditation

> *The miracle comes quietly into the mind*
> *that stops an instant and is still.*
>
> —*A Course in Miracles*

The practice of meditation can help us learn to stop and be in the present moment by bringing our awareness to our breath. It can teach us to find peace in each moment. Meditation is simply a time to quiet our minds and still our thoughts, a time to become centered and balanced. It is a time when we connect with a deeper place in ourselves, God, our souls, our hearts, our inner spirits or the higher energies of the universe.

Meditation has become more popular in the West since the 1970s, and there are hundreds of books that can teach you the many ways to meditate. Many of my books include meditation instructions, so I won't repeat them here. Workshops and retreats are offered just about everywhere. You can't go into a local health food store without seeing posters and advertisements for upcoming events that teach meditation.

Meditation can bring us to that deeper spiritual connection

that fills the empty space inside. This space is often referred to as spiritual deprivation, spiritual longing or the "God hole."

If you are new to meditation, lessons are a good way to begin. Find a teacher or a group. Ask around. You will be amazed at how many people will have suggestions for you. It's always helpful to practice regularly with an ongoing weekly group.

Experiment with different forms of meditation. See what feels right for you. Take time in solitude to give yourself the gift of developing a daily practice for which you take time, no matter what else is going on in your life.

> ### Meditation Tip
> It can be helpful to imagine a feather gently floating as you breathe in and out. Watch the feather as it drifts up with your out breath and drifts down with your in breath.

LETTING GO AFFIRMATION

*Healing is accomplished the instant the sufferer
no longer sees any value in pain.*

—*A Course in Miracles*

When we can learn to let go of our pain, as well as everything that we are holding on to that is keeping us stuck, joy begins to find its rightful place in our hearts. We become lighter and lighter to the extent of our willingness to let pain and suffering take their own natural course. And the more we let go, the clearer our futures become. Doors that we thought once closed to us begin to open. Opportunities appear everywhere, and we discover our true purposes.

*Today I choose to be open to
everything life presents to me, letting go
of all that is keeping me from
my joy and purpose.*

CHAPTER

2

My Dark Nights
of the Soul

We are all wounded by life.
We can all benefit from healing.
Some of us show it outwardly more than
others, but no one escapes bruising.
To live is to be hurt, and—sometimes inadvertently,
sometimes not—to hurt others, even those
closest to us. The fantasy that somehow we can
get through life pain-free is just that:
a phantasm of the mind; a mirage.

—Rabbi Sanford Ragins

Every flower must grow
through dirt.

—ANONYMOUS

Sometimes we hear an inner voice that screams so loudly that we must listen to it. It might appear to be an actual voice, a dream or some kind of sign. It might come to us as an inner knowing, the simple knowledge that it is time for change, that it might be time to follow another path. Perhaps we know we must do something now, or we feel directed to a change we don't want to make: a new career, a change of lifestyle, a letting go of a relationship. The call can be so very strong that no matter how painful it might be to make this change, we feel we have no choice.

A friend once told me he heard it as a wave that kept pouring over him, telling him to come along, come along, come along until he had no choice but to follow the calling. Responding to the message to serve God, he left everything he had and everyone he knew, and joined a monastery. In the end, when he surrendered to the call, he was very content with his decision.

My own soul searching, my struggle for self-understanding, independence and purpose, sometimes appeared as a loud, confident *Yes!* other times as a very weak, meek *No* and once as a roaring *Stop!*

I was born in Boston and named Ruth Lois Haase after my grandmother on my mother's side. Because there was already a Ruth Haase in our family, my parents decided to call me Lois, a name I didn't feel comfortable using. My father's job took our family to Detroit, Michigan, when I was two and a half years old, and a few years after our move, the Second World War broke out. We could get only a one-year lease when we rented a house and we had to move at the end of each lease period so that the soldiers coming home from the war could receive first priority for housing. Consequently, we moved at least four times from the time I was in kindergarten through the fourth grade.

Still, my memories of life in Detroit are very happy ones. There were lots of children in our neighborhood and there was always something to do. It was a very carefree, confident time in my life. Then, right before I turned ten years old, my father lost his job, and my family decided to move back to Boston. I had to leave all my friends behind. At the same time, I had a very strong urge to be called by my real name. I remember being absolutely sure that I wanted to be called Ruth. I wouldn't compromise. The timing was perfect because we were moving to a new place. The only people who knew me by the name Lois were my relatives and the people who knew me in Detroit.

At first, my parents didn't take me seriously when I announced my plan, and they continued to address me as Lois. Stubbornly and persistently, I refused to answer when they called me Lois. My family gradually trained themselves to think of me in this new way.

We had to move three more times to three other towns in Massachusetts during my fifth grade, because my father continued to change jobs. In all, I attended three different schools for the fifth grade and a fourth one for the sixth grade. As a result, my courage went underground for many years, I became quite shy and self-conscious, and it was very difficult for me to make new friends.

Our last move was to Brookline, Massachusetts, a town that was known at that time to be the home of well-to-do families. My father was unable to find work, and my uncle finally got him a very low paying job in the stockroom of a shoe factory. We had very little money and were fortunate to be able to rent the second floor of a two-family house in an upscale neighborhood. All the other homes were occupied by single families who were far better off financially.

I always felt inferior to the other students, and I remember my mother's excitement when she was able to buy six new school dresses for me for $1.00 each at a bargain store. The only time I felt good about what I was wearing was when I received a "care package" from my cousin Joanie, who lived in a fancy single-family home in Washington, D.C. Her clothes came from an upscale department store and they still had the labels inside!

Once in Brookline, my mother changed. Perhaps because my father lost his job and now we were struggling, she wanted to put up a good front and look as if we fit in with the neighbors. She wanted me to be like other girls who curled their hair and played with dolls. I was still the tomboy who loved to climb trees, play ball and shoot marbles.

I walked the two miles to school in those days, passing by homes that had bowling alleys in their basements and Cadillacs in their driveways. My father couldn't afford a car until I was almost seventeen. By then, many of the girls I knew had been given their own cars when they turned sixteen. I felt insecure, inferior and not as good as they were.

There was always alcohol in my house because my father was a heavy drinker. When I was around fifteen or sixteen years old, my cousins and I were allowed to join the adults on special occasions such as Thanksgiving or Chanukah and have a drink of our choice. I felt very grown-up and enjoyed being included with the adults. And I immediately loved the taste and the warm feeling I got from the alcohol. I began drinking at parties, and for the first time I felt relaxed in social situations. I finally felt as good as, as pretty as, and as smart as the other girls. By the end of my senior year in college, I was a daily drinker.

I started a greeting card company while in college and continued to build it when I graduated. Marrying one year after graduation, I continued my daily drinking—only now I became sneaky about it. I would pour one glass of scotch while making supper, going often into the kitchen to "check how dinner was coming along" while actually refilling my glass so it looked like I was only having one drink. Dinner was often very late in those days!

Eventually, my husband and I had three children, and he soon joined me in my greeting card company, and it continued to grow. Because we had our own business, I could come and go as I pleased, and I was always there when my children came home from school.

My drinking increased until I was up to almost a fifth a day. In the back of my mind I thought, *I can stop whenever I want*, but I knew I was lying to myself. I tried to stop. For the last five years of my drinking, I tried. I would wake up each morning and promise myself I wouldn't drink that day. But later I would leave work, and my car—as if it had a life of its own—would pull into a different package store each day. So pervasive was my shame that I thought that if I went into the same one, day after day, the clerk might think I had a drinking problem!

Somewhere deep inside me, my soul was screaming for help. I heard my own inner voice screaming *Stop!* over and over again, but I just couldn't. In the last months of my drinking, I would buy just a pint in the afternoon and promise myself I would only have one drink from it. When the pint was empty my resolve was empty as well, and I rushed out to the package store before it closed so I could buy another one. Once home again, I would drink until I passed out, then wake up in the middle of the night and finish whatever was left in my glass because, as my daily mantra went, "I'm not going to drink tomorrow."

I had arrived at a place in my life where I hated myself so much I could not continue to live the way I was living. I thought I was the worst mother, the worst wife and the worst daughter in the entire world. The emptiness I felt, the feeling that something was always missing, has been called a hole in the soul, or the dark night of the soul. My enemy was alcohol. My dark night of the soul was the years I could not stop drinking.

During the years of my daily drinking, I struggled repeatedly with trying to understand and know God, questioning whether there even was a God and desperately seeking meaning and purpose in my life. While I dearly loved my three children and my work, somewhere inside of me I always felt that I was meant to do more, but I had no understanding of what the "more" could be. I always had a yearning, a craving, as if something were missing, and I had no idea where to find it.

I actually felt as if I were in a dark hole during the years I could not stop drinking. Each day started with renewed hope that today would be different—I wouldn't drink—until the time when my car seemed to head automatically to a package store. I felt alone in my misery. I felt my only friend was my bottle, and how could I give that up?

This emptiness and longing has also been described as spiritual deprivation. We feel a longing, a craving, and we try to satisfy it with everything from alcohol and drugs, to food and sex, to gambling and thrills, only to find that while we might feel better temporarily, the pain always returns. In 1961, in a letter to Bill Wilson, cofounder of Alcoholics Anonymous, Carl Jung described addiction as "the equivalent, on a low level, of the spiritual thirst . . . for wholeness."

Our family had all the material things: a nice home, a boat and two cars. On the surface, everything looked fine. But deep inside I knew it wasn't. I no longer just wanted to drink every day, I *had* to drink every day. I could not stop.

After many years of struggling, becoming more and more depressed, I went to a psychiatrist who prescribed a variety of drugs for my condition, but I continued to drink while I took the pills. One morning, after taking my children out to eat the night before, I said to my son, "I have to go out and get dog food." He responded, "We already did, last night." I had no memory of going to the store, let alone driving home—a condition called a "black-out." I was now driving my children while in a blackout. Yet even this frightening realization was not enough to make me stop. However, soon after this incident, I could no longer live with myself because of all the guilt, shame and self-hate that I felt.

In deep anguish, I finally opened to the gift of desperation and joined a twelve-step recovery program. I reached for the phone and called for help. I began going to self-help groups with others who had gone through what I had experienced, people who couldn't stop drinking and were able to turn their lives around. These people were smiling, and they were full of joy. They were loving and supportive. They gave me their telephone numbers and said to call. They told me that by helping me they were helping themselves. That was how they stayed sober. I finally had found a new way of life. I began to discover what I had to do to become free of all the unhappiness, self-pity, self-consciousness and shame I carried deep within me. This new way of life began to unfold, to teach me how to live as light as a feather and find a new purpose in my life.

By now I was finally desperate enough to take the advice of people who had suffered as I had suffered but had learned to stop drinking. They suggested that I ask for help from a "power greater than myself." I was ready to try anything, even though I still didn't believe in God. I prayed, "If there is a God, you will understand, and if there isn't, it doesn't matter; but please, keep me away from a drink and a pill and the desire for a drink and a pill."

God does not always come in the form that we can recognize. God spoke to me through the people who were in recovery—

people who knew my pain, despair and hopelessness—because they had been there. People who knew that in order to stay sober themselves they had to help another suffering alcoholic.

Psychotherapist and author Marion Woodward writes, " . . . at the very point of vulnerability is where the surrender takes place—that is where the god enters. The god comes through the wound."[1] That's exactly the way it happened for me. The miracle happened! I was able to go through a day without a drink; and then two; and then ten. I would still pick up a drink after ten days or three weeks for a while, but the days were increasing between my drinks and I began to feel a bit better.

I came to believe in a power greater than myself, this God. I knew that on my own I could not stop drinking. Something greater than myself was working. I began to learn a whole new way of life.

When I finally did pray to the God that I did not believe in, relief came, and in time my desire to drink was miraculously lifted. It was enough to prove to me that I was not God. Years of pain and struggle gradually ended, and I had a spiritual awakening. It brought me to a new purpose, one that I could never have imagined for myself.

While I was in college I wrote a poem. It was not a very good poem, but I remember it to this day because it came from all the pain I felt while struggling to understand life and my place in it.

There's something I have to do—
An urge eating inside of me;
And until I find out what it is,
I shall never, never be free.
In the darkness of my thoughts
I sink within my sins,
In the struggle to know myself
And just where to begin.

As it turned out I did find a deep commitment to helping others. One evening, when I had been sober for seventeen days, I met a man who sat in his chair shaking. He was in such need of a drink. I remember looking at him with a huge smile and telling him to hang in there. "It's worth it," I said. "It works!" I'll never forget the feeling of joy I had in sharing that with this man. I had something to give after all! I had a purpose! That feeling has never changed.

Andrew Post writes that there is no greater reward in life than the sight of a shining smile after a waterfall of tears, and knowing that you were in part responsible for the transition. When I reach out to someone newly sober, or someone going through a difficult time, my heart fills with such gratitude. Over the following years I began the process of finding joy and a new purpose through the twelve steps of recovery, meditation and studying many of the major religions. All this in search of myself. I was clearing my mind of all old, misguided concepts, letting go of negative judgments about myself and others, and opening my heart to invite God into my life. Over time I learned the truth. The answers aren't "out there"; they are in our hearts, just where the creator put them.

The Ultimate Test

Everything I learned in the previous years was tested on October 12, 1992. On that Monday morning I was giving myself the gift of leisure and planned to take the day off to plant bulbs. I hadn't meditated yet, and I remember seeing that the time was 8:22 A.M. when the phone rang. It is very rare that I take a phone call before I meditate. A call from one of my children is the only exception.

"It's Bob," Sandy said, handing me the phone.

"Hi!" I said.

"I can't concentrate," he said. "I can't read. I'm too far behind. I have a paper that I have to turn in today and I'm nowhere near ready. I have to pass it in at 11 A.M. It's part of a team project," he went on to explain, "and I don't have anything valuable to contribute to the team. My contribution's a nothing. It's so nothing. Maybe I should be working at some mindless job. Maybe I shouldn't even be here in grad school. And I shouldn't be talking to you now. I shouldn't be taking so much time. I don't have time for this. I should be studying. Oh, God! I've already been on the phone for fifteen minutes.

"And I lost my Visa card. I have to call it in missing. I need to be studying and finishing my paper and calling Visa and finals are coming up in three days, and I can't concentrate and I have to get

A's or B's or my company won't pay for my courses, and I know I can't get A's or B's because I can't study. I can't read. I can't concentrate. I don't even remember what I'm reading!

"I haven't been able to sleep for two and a half weeks," he rambled on with hardly a breath between sentences. "I was up 'til two in the morning with the project, and I got up at 6 A.M. to study, and I haven't even been able to do anything today."

Somewhere in here I heard him crying.

"It's okay," I told him. "You'll be okay. Just slow down and take time to get yourself together." I assured him he was bright and that his paper sounded good, and I scoffed at the idea of a mindless job. I remember asking him if he was drinking a lot of Coke, to which he answered that he was. I suggested that the caffeine might be making him so agitated and keeping him awake.

"Are you swimming and exercising regularly?" I was groping, searching for some way to help.

"No, I'm not, but I'll try to fit a swim in if the pool is open by the time I finish my last class. Michele has been so understanding," Bob went on. Michele was his fiancée, and they were planning to be married the next July. She was going out with her mother to look for her gown that week.

"She has been so terrific," he said. "I was crying last night, and that was the first time that I let her see me cry."

During the entire conversation I pictured my son the way that I had last seen him in his new apartment only six weeks earlier. Then, he was strong and handsome, sure of himself and mature in so many ways, and I was so proud of him. His life felt so rich to me, so full of promise. He was well liked by everyone and loved by many. He had been president of his fraternity and interfraternity council. I even loved the way he dressed. He had great taste in clothes. He gave the appearance of a young man with great energy. That was the young man I had just visited.

"And there's something else I haven't said," he added.

I held my breath, sensing this was important.

"I had that thought again," he continued in a smaller, more distant, little boy voice, after a pause.

My heart stopped as he jolted me with his statement.

"What?"

"I'm thinking about 'doing it' again." He spoke barely above a whisper in a voice higher pitched than his usual voice.

I remember barely breathing.

"There's a bridge. With a parking lot under it."

I had been taught, years ago when I was involved with the counseling of alcoholic and chemically dependent women, always to ask the question, "Do you know how you are going to do it? Do you have a plan?" I had also been taught to ask if the person was serious. And if the answer was yes, to immediately call the police. You believe them. You always take them seriously.

"Are you serious?" I asked. It was almost as if I were reading my lines. Saying the appropriate words, as if I were in a play or a movie. I was reciting the questions and waiting for the correct answers in a space detached from reality. I say this. He says that. That's fine. Everything is going to be fine. Mother will find the right words to say, and her twenty-nine-year-old son will listen and do exactly what she suggests, and everything will be fine.

"No," Bob said. "I just thought about it."

He gave me the correct answer.

"That's right, dear," I breathed to myself.

I knew at least part of the reason for my son's stress. Bob was highly respected by the company for which he worked. They had given him a two-year leave of absence and were paying for the courses required to earn an MBA at Carnegie Mellon University if he earned no less than a B grade. In return, Bob would be obligated to work for his company after graduation for a minimum of two years. It seemed to be a golden time in his life now.

On the phone, he repeated to me that he couldn't concentrate. He couldn't study.

"Exams begin in only three days!" he shouted.

He went over and over the same words.

And again he was crying.

Somewhere in here my son said, "Mom, I'm almost thirty years old. When will this stop? Will this ever stop!? Will it ever get better?"

I suggested that he get a new therapist and find a good support group. He agreed. I then suggested that he get on his knees and pray for help to have his fear removed.

Bob said that he was doing that right there and then. He admitted that he had never gotten on his knees before. He was really doing it! He had reached a bottom but was willing to do everything he could to get through this terrible pain. I felt so encouraged by his willingness.

"Do you have a God bag?" I asked. This was the last suggestion I could think of.

"No," answered my son.

"Well, get a paper bag and write the word 'God' or 'higher power' or 'HP' on it, whichever makes you more comfortable," I suggested, as I had hundreds of times to other people. It was advice I followed myself. "Then write down all your fears and put them in the bag. Every time a fear comes up for you, know that you have that fear in the God bag. Know that you have turned it over. You don't have to worry about that any more. God, or your higher power, is handling it. There's nothing else you have to do about it."

He agreed to do this as well.

Before we hung up, I said, "I have only one errand to do this morning, and I will be back by 10:30 at the latest. I gave him my complete assurance that I would be available for him all day.

"Please call me if I can be of any help! I won't call you in case you're studying. I don't want to interrupt your concentration."

"Okay. Have to go, Mom." He sounded more energized, more directed.

"I'll call Visa first and report the lost card and then finish my paper." He promised he would call me during the day if he needed to talk.

"Thanks, Mom." He assured me he was okay. "I love you."

"I love you, too, honey. I love you, too."

I remember the clock showing 9:10 A.M. We had been talking more than forty-five minutes. The conversation had gone so well! I felt power flow through the telephone lines. I actually felt power in my arm and hand holding the phone, and I thought we had made a strong connection. I could picture the telephone wires connecting his phone and my phone and our hands and hearts. The power connected us. I remember sitting up straighter in bed, knowing that I was receiving strength from my higher power, and I was passing it on to my son.

Three years earlier we had shared a frighteningly similar conversation. That time fear had filled my body, and I felt hardly able to breathe. I remember my heart beating wildly, my knees getting weak. I paced the floor, questioning myself over and over as to whether I should fly or drive to Philadelphia, where he was living at the time.

That time, three years earlier, when Bob was in a deep depression, he told me he had pictured speeding up to 100 miles an hour and aiming his car into a tree. He came through that terrible time with the help of a very fine therapist and his family and friends. Now, this time, he sounded less intense. I felt certain that his last experience had helped him grow. He had come so far. He had worked so hard.

Bob often called me when he was in a stressful place. We were both in recovery from the effects of alcoholism in the family. We both spoke the same "recovery" language and sometimes just hearing phrases such as "Easy does it," or "Let go, let God," or being reminded to get to a support group meeting could turn a rough day into a pleasant one.

Before he sought professional help that first time, he would often call me at 5:30 A.M., too full of fear to get out of bed. He was afraid to face his day. He said I had a calm and soothing voice. I would talk gently with words of encouragement, affirmation and hope, trying to help him to connect with God, or a higher power. He would finally get up and struggle through another day until he could do it no longer. Finally, he gave up and followed his father's and my advice: He took a leave of absence from his high-pressure job, returned home and sought professional help for his pain and depression.

I believed this time he was reaching out, just as he had done before. I thought that this was another time where I would encourage and affirm him, until he got through the tough period. He had done so well before! He could find a new therapist, a new support group. It had worked before. There was no reason that it shouldn't work again. This time his future was even brighter: He was engaged to be married and had his fiancée and good friends around him.

I remember feeling reassured as I went about my planting that beautiful October day, still keeping the phone with me at all times. I never shook the thought that Bob was with me and that he was going to call any second. I checked the phone every once in a while, making sure it was working. I hadn't heard from him all day. At some point, between four and five o'clock, I double-checked the phone again, making sure the battery light was still on. I had placed the phone on a blanket and wondered if it was so well cushioned that perhaps I might not hear it ring.

The phone finally rang around five o'clock. I can't remember who it was, but I do remember being grateful that it was working. Good. He can call when he is ready.

I went in to make supper, feeling Bob's presence strongly, wishing he would call. After dinner, I sat down with a book that had just arrived in the mail that morning entitled *Handbook of Affective Disorders*. I had been attracted to this particular book like a magnet. I immediately looked up endorphins, serotonin and neurotransmitters, all the things I had been so strongly drawn to study for so many years. I wanted to find the answers; to help people still suffering from chemical imbalances. I knew the answers lay in the genes, our environment, the food we eat or don't eat, how our bodies process our food, stress and chemical imbalances. What else? I kept searching. It seemed as if I kept reading the same things over and over again, always reaffirming that I was in the right direction. The answers appeared to be too simple. There must be more. And I kept on reading.

I began making notes. I was getting ready to call Bob. *Turkey.* I kept reading the word "turkey" over and over again. Eat turkey to restore the balance of serotonin for feelings of well-being. I wrote down, "Eat more turkey."

If he didn't call me soon, I was going to call and tell Michele to make sure Bob ate more turkey. I was very nervous by now. It felt as if I were experiencing the longest day of my life. The last words of our conversation that morning kept coming back to me, sustaining me through my fears, convincing me that Bob was all right: "Thanks, Mom. I love you." His voice had been firm and upbeat.

"I love you too, Honey. I love you, too."

Suddenly the phone rang, jarring me out of a deep concentration. It was Michele, Bob's fiancée. The time was around 7 P.M.

"Hello, Ruth," she said. She sounded fine, with her Pennsylvania accent that usually made me smile.

"How are you? Ruth . . . ?" There was a hesitation in her voice. "Ruth, how did you find Bob this morning?" Her voice took on a high pitch.

"What do you mean?" I asked, my brain racing around the morning conversation I had had with my son, wondering how much to share, wondering what to say. How much had he told her? How much did he want her to know?

"Well," I said. "He was stressed. He was really stressed. He was full of anxiety."

"Ruth, I don't know how to tell you this, but Bob . . . Ruth . . . Oh, Ruth, I am so sorry to tell you this. Oh, Ruth! Bob's dead. I am so sorry!"

She began sobbing.

There was a long pause. I just stood there with the phone in my hand. Something inside me knew she was telling me the truth. Everything seemed to dim.

My pause felt like it was forever. Time just floated slowly by.

"What do you mean?" I said. "Tell me."

"Ruth, I'm so sorry. Ruth, I'm so sorry to have to tell you this. I wish I didn't have to be telling you this. I am so sorry." She was sobbing. "Ruth, someone from the coroner's office called me. He said Bob had jumped from a bridge. He's dead, Ruth. He's dead. Bob's dead, Ruth."

There was a long pause. My hands felt warm. My chest felt warm. The room was engulfed in stillness.

"Ruth, are you all right?"

"No," I said. "I'm not all right." My mind was racing with everything and with nothing. *What do I do now?* I thought.

"When did they call?" *So what*, I thought. *Why are you even asking this?*

"About a half hour ago."

"Oh, Michele. How are you? Where are you?"

I think I stood up when the phone rang. I remember it seemed dark. There was only one muted light on. I remember standing and holding the phone, looking down and being aware that I was wearing paint-spotted jeans. I felt very thin. I was not really sure if my legs were strong enough to hold me up. I remember that my knees were kind of bent and I felt weak, but I really could still stand up and that surprised me. In fact everything surprised me. I was aware that the phone was in my hand. I was aware of my breath and the time that I was taking to breathe, as if I were in slow motion. I was taking the time to wait a few seconds, to think of what to say and what to do next. I didn't think I could stand up another moment, that my legs could hold me up any longer. I remember thinking that this was too much for me to handle.

"Give me a moment, Michele. Please. Just give me a moment," I remember whispering. I sat down. I remember sitting there a few minutes. I really didn't know what to do right then. I still had the notebook in front of me with my notes in it.

"Ruth, are you all right?" She asked again.

I repeated, "No. I'm not all right. I'm not all right at all," in a low, deep whisper. It felt as if I were pushing my breath out of my mouth to make the words happen. My voice sounded as if it were coming from far away.

"I'll fly in as soon as possible," I said. "I'll be there tonight if I can."

I found myself going over and over the conversation I had with my son in my mind for weeks and months to come. It's easy enough to say that one shouldn't dwell on something that's in the past. It's easy enough to know that one shouldn't replay painful experiences over and over. Oh, but it's so much harder to follow this advice. And what is even more difficult to learn is that there are some instances in life, some very rare, horrible, agonizing experiences in life, that, no matter how many times we try to figure them out, no matter how many times we go over them, cannot ever be fully explained or resolved.

Friends tell us not to feel guilty. Experts and therapists tell us not to blame ourselves. We can read all the books written on the subject and know that there are a multitude of "should's" and "should not's." But for most of us, there is an innate need to find the truth. There is an innate need to look at each straw in the haystack. To hold it and turn it and examine it . . . to reexamine it . . . to touch it and smell it and hear it . . . to look at it—again—searching for the missing pieces . . . searching for clues . . . or just one clue . . . trying to find the answer to such looming questions as "Why?" and "What could I have done differently?" To know every part of it before becoming willing to put it down.

Was there something I had missed? Was there a tone that would have told me more if I could only have heard it? Did I talk too much and not listen well enough? I remember jumping in at one point and sharing how similar something was for me. Maybe if I hadn't done that . . . maybe if I had only paused instead. Maybe he had more to say. Maybe there was something else that would have come from him that I had blocked by my own sharing. And yet . . . I thought I was helping with my sharing. I thought I was helping by letting him know that I knew how he felt. That I had felt that way, too, and that it passes. Oh, God, the agony of second-guessing!

Was my son crying at the beginning or did that come later?

Calls from the dean and the police soon followed. Bob had checked on his license that he wanted to be an organ donor, so a call came to get my permission. I had to find his father, who was traveling at the time, and call his two sisters with this heartbreaking news.

The next days and weeks were a blur of pain, of putting one foot in front of the other, going to Pittsburgh to bring him home, getting through the funeral, sitting with friends and relatives during *shiva* (the Jewish time of mourning) at his father's house. I remember the pain was so great at times I felt as if I couldn't breathe or move. Yet, other times I felt light and soft, as if I were wrapped in a cocoon of cotton, being held and guided and taken care of at all times.

This was the darkest time of my life. Still, there were moments of brilliant light. I remember looking out the window on the bright, sunny morning of my son's funeral, seeing the magnificent rich colors in the October trees. I thought, *How could he have done this? Never to see this earth again?* Until that moment, from the time that I heard the news of his death, a fear had been hovering around the sidelines of my thoughts that I could not push away. Bob and I were alike in many ways. What if I decided to take my life? What if some uncontrollable force became so strong that I would have no choice? I knew then, on that sunny, colorful, horribly painful, sad, mournful day that I was grateful to be alive.

I was grateful that I had nineteen years of sobriety, and I had learned how to take care of myself. I was grateful that I now believed in a God of love and goodness, an energy and power which I knew would take care of me if I simply reached out and up. I was grateful for my fourteen years of meditation, which I knew would bring me peace. I was grateful for friends who didn't know what to say but sent beautiful cards and letters, and for the warmth and love of my daughters. I was grateful for my partner of nineteen years, and for the support, love, understanding and comfort I was receiving from her.

This is not to say that the pain went away. I think it was months before I laughed, and then I felt immediately guilty. I sat in darkness for hours and stared at nothing. I had the gift of a wonderful therapist who charged me half price and saw me twice a week for four months. She sat with me when I couldn't speak, or when I made a weak attempt at explaining the ponderousness of my feelings.

I had learned enough to know that I had to feel everything there was to feel—numbness, pain, anger, guilt. I remember the good intentions of my brother when he said that I should not be so stubborn, that I should take some tranquilizers. I knew medication would simply prolong my suffering. I did everything I knew how to do to get through this time. I wrote and wrote and wrote, pouring out all my feelings into the computer. I went to Compassionate Friends, a wonderful support group for people who have lost children and siblings.

Two weeks after Bob died, I facilitated a workshop that had been planned months earlier. The proceeds were going to a charity, and I decided, no matter how I felt, that I would like to go through with the workshop. I drove the hour and a half to the site in silence, feeling numb and empty, wondering where I would get the energy to open my mouth, let alone put thoughts together to make sense.

As soon as the workshop began, I shared what was going on in my life. I had to say the words to release them, as they were sitting so heavily in my chest. The silence in the room was immediate, respectful and yet not oppressive. I could feel people were barely breathing, not quite sure how or even whether to respond. At first I thought I had made a monstrous mistake in revealing something so personal and painful. Still, I knew this was the only way I could continue. If I were not honest about where I was in this moment, how could I possibly teach about mindfulness, which is about being fully alive in the moment.

One woman had to leave the workshop before it ended. She mouthed an apology to me, saying she had a previous engagement. Later, when I went out to my car, there was a note under my windshield wiper. I later found the source and have kept a copy of it ever since in my office where I can see it. The note said, "I will instruct you and teach you in the way you should go, Psalms 32:8."

And that's exactly what has happened. I did find a purpose in all this pain. In time, I facilitated workshops at conferences for Compassionate Friends and the American Foundation for Suicide Prevention. Each time I shared my pain, and how I got through it, I felt a little lighter. I was turning my pain into purpose and helping to light the way for others to heal.

I believe God uses our pain to help lighten the burdens of others who are in situations similar to the ones we have experienced. Barbara, a dear friend of mine, says that God is an opportunist. He takes every opportunity to bring good out of evil. We simply need to respond to God's gentle nudging.

I also wrote a book—*STOP! Do You Know You're Breathing? Simple Techniques for Parents and Teachers to Reduce Stress and Violence at Home and in the Classroom.*[2] I did not plan this book. It just came, as the gentle nudging about which Barbara spoke. After a few years of my own healing, I knew I had to try to help students reduce their stress, to let them know they did not have to be perfect and to offer ways that would increase their self-esteem so that they would not suffer as my son had. I went to schools and conferences and taught teachers simple exercises to pass on to the kids to release stress, and I also taught these techniques directly to the students. Where did the book come from? Where did the ideas come from? I believe I was inspired as we all are when we are open to God's will for us. Judaism says that the very purpose of existence is the continuous perfecting of the universe. I believe there are times for all of us when we receive a gentle nudging from God, and there are other times that God hits us over the head with a two-by-four to help us move forward. Sometimes we move easily and other times with effort, forcing one foot in front of the other. But move forward we must, or we will stay locked in the dark night of the soul.

Our own reaching out to the heavy hearts of people in pain lossens the chains that keep us in the prison of our own pain. As feathers float on the lightest breeze, our gentle words, our soft touch, our compassionate presence can be the breeze that stirs the hearts of fellow sufferers. Throughout this book you will learn simple techniques to find peace and joy in your heart and a new purpose in your life.

Take some time now to examine your life and identify times when you have gone through difficult situations:

- How did you get through these experiences?
- Did they make you stronger?
- What can you share with others to give them hope?
- Is there more you have to do to come to a place of peace and healing?

The Heart-Lightening Process
Step 2:

BRING YOUR FULL AWARENESS TO WHATEVER
IS HAPPENING IN THE MOMENT

*Everything is shown up by being
exposed to the light, and whatever is exposed
to the light itself, becomes light.*

—ST. PAUL (EPH. 5:13)

When we *stop,* we can get in touch with what we are feeling in the present moment. We begin to do it by bringing our awareness to whatever is going on in the present moment, including our thoughts and our feelings. Once we notice them, we become mindful of how our thoughts affect our feelings. Through the simple act of changing our thoughts, we can change how we feel. Then we can let the lower energy feelings go and replace them with higher energy feelings; we can learn to have thoughts of joy and love.

Does what you are feeling in the present moment bring you to higher energy states of joy or peace? Or are you in lower energy states of fear or anger? Simply notice your emotion. Your purpose in this moment is nothing more than to notice what you are experiencing. Imagine you have a gentle witness on your shoulder, detached and nonjudging, simply observing whatever is going on.

An essential part of finding and fulfilling your purpose is focusing on what is important to you. The following story illustrates our need to develop awareness.

A Native American and his friend were in downtown New York City, walking near Times Square in Manhattan. It was during the noon lunch hour and the streets were filled with people. Cars were honking their horns, taxicabs were squealing around corners, sirens were wailing, and the sounds of the city were almost deafening. Suddenly, the Native American said, "I hear a cricket." His friend said, "What? You must be crazy. You couldn't possibly hear a cricket in all of this noise!"

"No, I'm sure of it," the Native American said. "I heard a cricket."

"That's crazy," said the friend.

The Native American listened carefully for a moment and then walked across the street to a big cement planter where some shrubs were growing. He looked into the bushes, beneath the branches, and sure enough, he located a small cricket. His friend was utterly amazed.

"That's incredible," said his friend. "You must have super-human ears!"

"No," said the Native American. "My ears are no different from yours. It all depends on what you're listening for."

"But that can't be!" said the friend. "I could never hear a cricket in this noise."

"Yes, it's true," came the reply. "It depends on what is really important to you. Here, let me show you."

He reached into his pocket, pulled out a few coins and discreetly dropped them on the sidewalk. And then, with the noise of the crowded street still blaring in their ears, they noticed

every head within twenty feet turn and look to see if the money
that tinkled on the pavement was theirs.

"See what I mean?" asked the Native American. "It all
depends on what's important to you."

~~~~~~

Awareness gives us power. We can experience how our thoughts precede our feelings. When we begin to watch our thoughts, we are awake to the fact that we create our own reality. We gain insight into what makes us tick.

Become aware of your body. Notice your tongue and what happens when you pay attention to it. Do you feel pain in places in your body where you are holding tension? Can you feel your heart beat? Are your hands warm or cool? Feel your chest rise and fall with each breath. These are just a few ways in which you can bring your awareness into the present moment, getting out of your head and away from all the thoughts that go on and on, blocking you from experiencing the now.

Meditation teacher and author Jack Kornfield illustrates this so well. He describes three types of individuals who have three different ways of entering a room where there is a party. The first person is in the wanting, grasping state and thinks, *Who's attractive? Where's the food?* The second type of person is in the state of aversion and sees what's wrong with everything. *He's a snob. The room is too cold. The music is too loud.* The third type of person is free. This person just goes into the room, accepting what is.[3]

Often we have to look deeply to see what is going on within

ourselves. We must bring to light that which is causing our heart to be heavy so that we can let it go. What type of person are you when you go to a party or enter a room full of strangers?

Remember, what we think is what we feel.

The source of your unhappiness might be a habitual pattern of thinking that pulls you down, such as blaming another so that you don't have to take responsibility for your feelings. The source might be an old, buried tape which originated with your father who asked, "Why can't you be as smart as your sister?"

Self-knowledge can lead to self-acceptance, which can lead to choice. Once we choose to give ourselves permission to feel all of who we are, opening ourselves to all of our feelings—even those of which we are not proud—we will see that this choice leads to freedom and freedom leads to a light heart.

Take time to notice the thoughts that precede your feelings. Are you coming from a place of love or fear?

There might be times that you cannot identify what you are feeling. There are times when you have no choice, when your emotions might be out of control. That's just the way it is and your feelings will eventually settle down. This can occur in a sudden accident, for example, when things happen so fast you become totally overwhelmed. It can happen when you fall in love! I was told once that falling in love is just that—falling—and we have no control over the feeling.

Mindfulness

If we are really engaged in mindfulness . . .
a joy will open our hearts like a flower, enabling
us to enter into the world of reality.

—Thich Nhat Hanh

There are many ways to meditate. The form I have been practicing for over twenty-five years and teaching for over twenty is insight meditation, also known as mindfulness. This is the practice of quieting down our thoughts and being fully present in each moment with full awareness of what is going on.

It can also be a spiritual practice. One can meditate and not be religious, and yet meditation is a part of most religions. Most important, it's a deeply personal experience.

One of my favorite teachers, who is also an author and retreat leader, Christina Feldman, tells us that "to undertake a period of meditation is to offer a gift to yourself. It is an act of caring for your own well-being and consciously nurturing inner connection. It is a time of exploring the most intimate relationship of your life, your relationship with yourself. It is helpful to approach these times with deep sensitivity and care so that they may be times of enrichment." She writes that grace is found in our capacity to listen inwardly and to trust in that listening.

Mindfulness brings us clarity and wisdom. I don't mean that we accept whatever is going on without further action. If someone is being abused, we do whatever we can to stop it. If a child is running out into the street, we run after her and pull her back. By being present with whatever is going on in the moment, we see what action, if any, needs to be taken.

We use the term "the practice of mindfulness" or "the practice of meditation" because it is simply that, a practice. Just as we practice the piano, dancing or anything that requires repetition to gain skills, we practice mindfulness by sitting with our breath. For one or more periods each day, we notice what takes us away from our breath, returning each time to our breath.

Thich Nhat Hanh teaches that it does not matter how many times we leave our breath, but how many times we come back to it. He teaches that the secret of meditation is to become conscious of each moment of our existence.

My favorite definition of mindfulness (or insight meditation) is from the Insight Meditation Society in Barre, Massachusetts: "Insight meditation is a simple and direct practice—the moment to moment investigation of the mind-body process through calm and focused awareness. Learning to experience from a place of stillness enables one to relate to life with less fear and less clinging. Seeing life as a constantly changing process, one begins to accept pleasure and pain, fear and joy and all aspects of life with increasing equanimity and balance. As insight deepens, wisdom and compassion arise. Insight meditation is a way of seeing clearly the totality of one's being and experience. Growth in clarity brings about penetrating insight into the nature of who we are and increased peace in our daily lives."[4]

The key word to my understanding mindfulness meditation is awareness. Awareness is consciousness, knowledge and wakefulness.

The purpose of mindfulness is to be fully awake and aware in each moment, to discover the essence of who we are, to get in touch with all the blocks that keep us from touching our inner spirits, listening to the guidance of our souls and feeling the joy in our hearts.

Bringing Meditation into Our Daily Lives

*Everything in our lives can help us
to wake up or to fall asleep, and basically
it's up to us to let it wake us up ... with awareness,
you are able to find out for yourself what causes
misery and what causes happiness."*

—Pema Chodron, Buddhist teacher and author

Meditation begins with a daily sitting practice. We stop all outside activity and sit quietly. As we develop the practice to stop and look inside, and it becomes more and more a part of our lives, we also find that we stop looking outside. Author, physician and teacher Deepak Chopra tells us, "Be willing to follow the clues of the spirit, meditate to find the pure silence within yourself, know that the goal of spirit is true and worth pursuing."

We can find joy and peace when we stop to examine the smallest leaf, look into the most intricate flower, watch a bumblebee flit from blossom to blossom, keep our focus on one single snowflake as it slowly falls to the ground. We become better listeners, less self-absorbed, more open to share.

Another way to meditate is to practice a slow meditative walk as you are going to and from your car. This can be a wonderful transition from work to home or vice versa, leaving work at work or concerns you have at home at home by being in the present moment. Rather than being off somewhere in your head, lost in your thoughts, thinking and planning, instead bring your full awareness to the present moment. Feel your feet in your shoes, touching the ground as your arms are swinging normally and your body is moving. You can feel joy when you actually experience the intricate movements of your body and realize the wonder of it.

Even on a crowded street or at a busy beach, walking meditation can help you slow down, become centered again and keep you in the present moment. This can bring you a deep sense of peace.

Some years ago, Buddhist meditation teacher Joanne Friday suffered a very bad car accident and was in extreme physical pain. When she walked to exercise, she muttered, "Why me? Why did this terrible thing happen to me?" Joanne was terribly depressed and exhausted by the end of each walk.

As she began practicing mindfulness meditation, however, she changed how she looked at the situation. She saw the magnificent sky and began to realize all the things for which she was grateful.

"It was pretty much a miracle that I was walking at all! Depending on where I chose to focus my mind, I would be absolutely euphoric when I finished my walk, or in pain. That is the fruit of the practice. If you concentrate on finding whatever is good in every situation, you will discover that your life will suddenly be filled with gratitude, a feeling that nurtures the soul."

BRINGING MINDFULNESS TO OUR THOUGHTS

*To be conscious that we are perceiving or thinking
is to be conscious of our own existence.*

—ARISTOTLE

Imagine something coming up in the future that makes you nervous. Perhaps you are taking an exam, speaking publicly or having an operation. Feel how your body responds to this thought. Are you holding your breath? Does your stomach tighten or turn over? Where do you hold your fears?

Now bring your attention to a time when you felt great joy. Again, feel how your body responds to this memory. Is there a different expression on your face? Is your body more relaxed? Is your breath different? By bringing our attention to these positive *and* negative feelings, the negative feelings tend to lose their power over us. When we open up to the awareness of the present moment, and breathe into it, the feelings of tension and fear wash away and we feel peace. Take time in solitude to study the way you respond to your thoughts and feelings. Be gentle and loving with yourself. This is a wonderful way to get to know yourself.

How many times have you been driving and suddenly realized that you didn't remember driving from one place to another? How often do you find yourself in a conversation suddenly realizing that you haven't heard part of what the speaker was saying to you? Your mind has been either off in a daydream, or wondering what you are going to say next, or judging what is being said to you. Maybe your mind "went away" remembering something in the past or worrying about something in the future. A daily practice of meditation helps develop concentration and focus. It helps train your mind to be in the moment, to bring your full attention to what is going on in the moment. You can become a better listener and friend by being totally present with another person.

The word *Budh* in the Indian Sanskrit language means "to wake up, to know." Buddha means "the Awakened or Enlightened One," and all Buddhist teachings try to share the Buddha's experience of awakening to truth. The Buddha discovered that the world was full of suffering and that there was a way to end suffering. Mindfulness, he taught, is the path to end suffering.

When we bring mindfulness into our lives we also become aware of the thoughts that create our suffering. We can see more clearly when we are holding on to anger, resentments, guilt and all other emotions that lead us to pain. We learn by experiencing the feelings that are connected with our thoughts, by observing the mind-body connection.

THE POWER OF NOTING

When we let go of our battles and
open our hearts to things as they are, then
we come to rest in the present moment. This is the
beginning and end of spiritual practice.

—JACK KORNFIELD, BUDDHIST TEACHER AND AUTHOR

There is a wonderful technique that is part of mindfulness called "noting." It is suggested that we learn to label our thoughts as they appear in our minds and then go back to our breathing. By labeling them, or naming them, we are acknowledging and accepting them, rather then resisting or fighting them. For example, when a thought or a plan comes into our mind, we simply say, "thinking" or "planning." For some reason I have yet to understand, the thoughts immediately lose their power over us and our minds becomes empty again, even if it is for a brief time before the next thought appears.

By practicing this technique during our daily meditation, we can learn to bring it to each moment of our day, which keeps us in the present moment.

Noting or labeling is a wonderful technique to use in solitude when you become disturbed by a mind that won't give you peace. When the "to do" list won't leave you alone, just say "thinking" or "busy mind," and watch the thoughts disappear. Jack Kornfield writes, "Naming the difficulties we encounter brings clarity and understanding and can unlock and free the valuable energy locked up in them."

It also works if you can't fall asleep at night. There was a time when my thoughts kept me awake for a long time. When I learned the noting technique, however, I finally found a way to stop my circular thinking. In the early days of our halfway house, we barely had enough money for food. I would wake up every morning around five o'clock, unable to fall back to sleep. My mind would go over and over the same problems. *How will we pay our bills? Where will we find enough beds for the women who need them?* I learned, to my relief, that it is impossible to have two thoughts at the same time. Therefore, when I breathed in, I thought the word "peace," and when I breathed out I thought the word "tension." If I was nervous about something I breathed in the word "faith" and breathed out the word "fear." Within minutes I was asleep again.

LETTING GO AFFIRMATION

And if not now, when?

—THE TALMUD

There is no better time than right now to stop and examine if we have any old grudges, any incomplete business, or any unfulfilled promises. These burdens weigh heavily in our lives, whether we are aware of it or not. Because many of us are so accustomed to carrying these burdens, we take their presence for granted.

We only have this present moment. We can't bring it back. If we make the most of it, follow the guidance of our hearts, we bring lightness to the moment and to each succeeding moment.

*Today I am looking deeply for
anything that remains unfinished in my life
and am taking the time to bring closure
when I do find something.*

CHAPTER

3

Opening Our Hearts

And now here is my secret,
a very simple secret; it is only with
the heart that one can see rightly;
what is essential is invisible
to the eye.

—*The Little Prince,*
Antoine-Marie-Roger de Saint-Exupery

Every decision, every choice, every thought,
word and action is an opportunity to consciously
create, and a statement of Who We Really Are.

—NEALE DONALD WALSH

W e hear phrases like the above all the time. But how can we open our hearts? Do they open simply because we decide to open? Or are there certain techniques we must learn to feel love in our hearts? Clearly, there are times when our hearts open spontaneously. It might happen for you, for example, when you see a baby smile for the first time, and your chest feels like it might burst. Or your heart might suddenly open with a feeling of strong compassion when you see a starving child on television.

Most of the time we are not even aware that our hearts are closed, and we go from day to day trying to get what we want so that we can be happy. Once we begin to look inside, however, we discover that we have what we need to open our hearts and feel love and joy more often. For Natalie, the process of opening her heart involved a long journey.

Natalie had tried two colleges after graduation from high school. The first time she studied physical therapy and then changed to psychology and sociology. She enjoyed making connections with people but felt nothing when she was studying or in the classroom. After attending the second college and dropping out, she moved to Nantucket, Massachusetts, where she met wonderful, supportive people. To pay the bills, she took jobs working as an estate manager and doing private home health care. She felt most comfortable and was the happiest when nurturing people.

When a friend encouraged her to go back to school, she applied to and was admitted into Harvard. She thought that once she arrived there everything would finally become clear for her. It would all come together. All her education would finally pay off. This time, she was determined to graduate and prove herself. But Natalie's bubble burst as her disappointment grew when none of her classes touched or motivated her. She looks back at her time at Harvard as a great experience, but not because of her books or lectures. Rather, she learned so much from the interesting people she met or from something a professor said that touched her deeply.

Again, she was sad and discouraged, and she decided to quit school, much to the dismay of her parents. They had always been supportive of her, but this time they did not understand her at all.

When the disaster of September 11, 2001, occurred, Natalie knew she didn't want to be in the city, so she decided to go back to the comfort of friends on Nantucket for a month to think. People on the island were holding religious vigils everywhere to honor and remember the victims of the attacks and their families. Natalie felt that rather than bringing them together, the religious vigils were separating people. She felt a strong desire to gather with other people and hold a vigil that was not religiously based. So, she called friends and put up fliers calling for a nondenominational community vigil on the beach. Amazingly, 250 people showed up! Natalie had never done anything like this before, and she felt something shift inside of her. It was a beautiful experience. She said a few words, as did others, and everyone sang. She felt, as was depicted in the movie Field of Dreams, *that if you believe it and speak it, they will come. Natalie knew that what drew people to her came out of her heart. "I opened my heart and people came," she recalled. "I had always thought I should be in my head."*

Seeing an ad for a new program based on spirituality and metaphysics, Natalie called to find out more about it and enrolled with the goal of becoming a counselor. Finally, she found what she had been looking for all these years. Now she is excited to get to class and when she is there, sits on the edge of her seat, thrilled with what she is learning. She wants more and more and more.

Because she had the courage to follow the path that laid itself out before her, Natalie knows that the love she needs and wants is already inside of her. "I found that I am able to heal when my heart is open," she says.

Take a moment now to stop. Breathe in and out naturally. This is the first step to a joyful heart.

Since we usually feel our emotions somewhere in the area of our chest, and because we know this is where our hearts lie, we have come to speak of our hearts as if they have feelings. Trying to imagine our hearts, a picture of something looking like a valentine might come into our minds. We use phrases such as:

- "Can you find it in your heart to forgive me?"
- "When she left him, it broke his heart."
- "You have warmed my heart."
- "She's so heartless."
- "She has a heavy heart," (or a light heart, or a broken heart, or a full heart).
- "He has no heart," or "He is heartless."

Words such as "I'm sorry," "Can I help?" or "I understand," can soften our hearts and ease years of pain. A simple smile can remove the wall between people who have been separated by anger. On the other hand, a sharp criticism, a sarcastic retort or a broken promise can harden our hearts, put walls up between people and shut them down for a long time.

You can probably remember a time when you were afraid, and you could feel your heart beat faster. Maybe you were called on in school to give an answer, and you hadn't done your homework; or a dog ran in front of your car, and you barely stopped in time. I know when I began public speaking, I was petrified. My hands were sweaty, my mouth was dry and I was sure the audience could hear my heart beat, it sounded so loud in my own ears. There were other times when my heart was so touched by someone's kindness that I felt it soften and expand; it radiated warmth throughout my body and my eyes filled with tears of love and gratitude. There is no question that our hearts are affected by our emotions.

The ancient Hebrews believed that the heart was the seat of wisdom and understanding, the inner personality, the whole gamut of emotional life, as well as the collective mind, or mind-set of the people, the mental heart as well as the fleshy heart.[1]

Many religions refer to the heart as the seat of the soul. Gary Zukav, author of the bestselling book *The Seat of the Soul,* writes that the soul is that part of us that is immortal. It is a positive, purposeful force at the core of our being. He suggests that the first step to knowing our soul is to recognize that we have a soul. Once we align our personality with our soul, we come from a place of authentic empowerment.

We believe that our hearts have qualities far beyond that of a muscle that pumps blood through our bodies and keeps us alive. We use the heart as a metaphor when we speak of the higher aspects of spiritual life—such as love, compassion and forgiveness. Now there is scientific research that seems to prove the philosophers, poets and mystics may have been right all along. They have told us since the beginning of recorded time that we should follow our hearts. The philosopher Pascal wrote, "We know the truth not only by reason but also by the heart."

Research by Doc Childre, founder of the Institute of HeartMath, says that he has proven that the heart actually has its own independent nervous system. Called "the brain in the heart," it can relay information, thereby creating a two-way communications system between the heart and the brain. This research claims that the heart also communicates with the rest of the body and is connected to our thoughts and to our senses. Research from the Institute of HeartMath says that the heart sends us emotional and intuitive signals to help govern our lives. It is capable of giving us messages that can have an impact on our decision-making, our health problems and the overall quality of our lives. The heart can feel emotion and can "think" and help us to live happier, more spiritual lives.[2]

HeartMath Institute researchers also discovered that the heart communicates with the brain and the rest of the body in three ways: neurologically (through the transmission of nerve impulses), biochemically (through hormones and neurotransmitters), and biophysically (through pressure waves). They also say that there is growing scientific evidence that the heart may communicate with the brain and body a fourth way: energetically (through electromagnetic field interactions). Neurocardiology, a new discipline that combines the study of the nervous system with the study of the heart, has emerged within the last twenty years.[3]

> Take a moment now to stop.
> Put your hand over your heart. This is where your joy lives.
> Can you feel it?

In the book *The Heart's Code,* well-known author and scientist Paul Pearsall writes that the heart thinks, remembers, communicates with other hearts, helps regulate immunity and contains stored information that continually pulsates through the entire body. Science has made new discoveries that suggest that "the heart thinks, cells remember, and that both of these processes are related to an as yet mysterious, extremely powerful, but very subtle energy with properties unlike any other known force." Pearsall calls this force "life energy" or "L" energy.[4]

So pervasive is "L" energy that indigenous peoples and ancient religious systems have given it over one hundred different names and base their healing systems on it. In India and Tibet, this energy is called *rana*. The Chinese call it *chi*, Polynesians call it *mana* and the Sufis call it *baraka*. Jews in the cabalistic tradition call it *yesod*, the Iroquois call it *orendam*, the Ituraea pygmies call it *megbe* and Christians call it the Holy Spirit.

"Many modern psychologists have dealt with and named 'L' energy," Pearsall writes. "They have used names such as 'the fifth force' and 'X' energy. Psychologist Wilhelm Riech called it 'organum,' Sigmund Freud called it 'libido' and Franz Anton Mesner (like biologist Luigi Galvani) called it 'animal magnetism.' Karl von Reichenbach called it 'odic forcem.' Psychologists in Russia used to call it 'biplasma.'

"In dealing with emotional development and distress, almost every form of psychotherapy has offered its own version of 'L' energy, which serves as a motivating life force."[5]

Pearsall has also done a great deal of research on the heart, conducting fascinating studies of people who have had heart transplants. He has found that many of the patients studied experienced changes in their tastes for food, music and other preferences. Many patients felt they knew about the person who had been the original owner of the heart. They knew details about the donor even though they had never met him or her.

One fascinating story about a young girl was reported by her therapist at a conference: "I have a patient, an eight-year-old girl who received the heart of a murdered ten-year-old girl. Her mother brought her to me when she started screaming at night about her dreams of the man who had murdered her donor. She said her daughter knew who it was. After several sessions with her, I just could not deny the reality of what this child was telling me. Her mother and I finally decided to call the police and, using the descriptions from the little girl, they found the murderer. He was easily convicted with evidence my patient provided: the time, the weapon, the place, the clothes he wore and what the little girl he killed had said to him. Everything the little heart transplant recipient reported that could be checked was completely accurate."[6]

The Judaic tradition believes that the heart is the crucible of a person's true essence.[7] The Sufis believed in the intelligence of the heart, the thought of the heart and the eye of the heart. They believed that only those who possessed an inner heart could heed and recall messages from the Divine. In the Koran, God or Allah speaks through Gabriel to Mohammed and states that the heart is the organ of discernment, and therefore the most valuable target of corruption.

The Upanishads, which comprise the oldest philosophical literature of the Hindus, declare that the Divine Being already resides in the secret cave of our hearts. Author Gail Godwin writes: "A powerful current of similar thinking and feeling connects the Upanishads with the later 'faiths of the heart,' ranging from the beliefs of the Islamic Sufis to the preachings of Meister Eckhart, the thirteenth-century Catholic founder of German mysticism (who was condemned as a heretic). The kernel of all these faiths is the same: The God who lives yonder is put aside for the God who is at home in the human heart and radiates his effects outward from that power source."[8]

If, as some religions believe, the heart is the seat of the soul, then what is the soul? Does it differ from the heart or are the two interchangeable?

The Egyptians believed in the *ba,* or the heart-soul, which was a spirit that survives death. When they began to believe in resurrection, they needed to preserve the physical body and began the process of mummification. All the internal organs except the heart were removed. As discussed in the first chapter, the Egyptians believed that in the next world the gods would weigh the heart against a feather to determine the balance of good and evil in an individual at the time of death.

We certainly know the heart is real as an organ. Now we see that the heart may also have a "brain." As far as the soul is concerned, we do know that we have the spirit of life in us, and when we stop breathing our life force leaves us. Whether we have a soul, something that lives on like a spirit in some form or another, is up to each of us to decide. It has been an ongoing debate between people of all faiths and will probably continue to be one.

What is a light heart? What makes for a heavy heart? And if our hearts ever do become as light as a feather, will our souls really live on forever?

Let's move on to discover how we can make our hearts lighter while we are alive and find more joy, balance, equanimity—even the ecstasy that mystics speak of.

It's obvious that if our hearts are full of anger, bitterness and grief, there is little room for love, compassion and joy. It might seem impossible to imagine how a person who has just been fired, or lost a loved one or has to put a pet to sleep can possibly feel joy. And, indeed, it's true that they can't if they are unwilling to let go of their pain. But with willingness, one can move forward.

Betty is a wonderful example of someone who has done just that. Betty thought her life was over when, many years ago, she lost someone very close to her. A next-door neighbor came over every day to be with Betty, sometimes just sitting with her, other times taking her out for a ride. Over time she learned the meaning of compassion from the next-door neighbor who spent so much time with her. Since then, Betty always tries to be there for others who are going through anything painful. She works at a nursing home a few days a week. Each week she visits a woman with Alzheimer's and leaves six gumdrops on her bureau. And each week the woman says, "Where did you get these? They are just wonderful!" And her face lights up with a huge smile.

Energy

How can we apply this information to our own lives? Let's start by looking at the power that words have in whether we are happy or not.

Words are energy. The power of the words that we think sends energy to our bodies. We *feel* the energy of the words that we think. Energy vibrates at different frequencies. If we think high-energy thoughts we feel light, joyful, loving. If we think low-energy thoughts we feel heavy, dark, unhappy, depressed.

There is a great deal of scientific research that proves this to be true. Brain scan studies show that when we think positive thoughts, our endorphins—the body's feel-good neurotransmitters—flow and we feel great. When we think negative thoughts, they stop flowing. It's as simple, or as complicated, as that.

Stephan Rechtschaffen, M.D., author and president of Omega Institute, writes that the rhythms of the heart are regulated by love. Love and positive feelings in the heart create a rhythm that spreads health and well-being throughout the body.[9] It has been proven over and over that giving and receiving care and compassion play a great role in our health and longevity. Thoughts such as gratitude, appreciation and acceptance raise our energy, giving us light hearts. Negative and judgmental thoughts, jealousy, and resentments are just a few of the emotions that deplete our energy, resulting in heavy hearts.

I have always been fascinated with the power of words and have written about them before in a number of my own books. Dr. Valerie Hunt is a scientist and a physiological researcher of human energy. In her book *Infinite Mind: Science of the Human Vibrations of Consciousness,* she writes, "As a result of my work I can no longer consider the body as organic systems or tissues. The healthy body is a flowing, interactive electrodynamic energy field. Motion is more natural to life than non-motion—things that keep flowing are inherently good. What interferes with flow will have detrimental effects."[10]

The image of a kitchen faucet can be very helpful to our understanding of this principle. Imagine a faucet that when turned on allows water to flow with a powerful force. Then, over the years, as the pipe becomes clogged or corroded, the water's force gradually becomes weaker and weaker until there is barely a trickle. That's exactly what happens to our power, our connection to a higher power, when we are clogged with anger, resentments, fear, self-pity and other negative, low-energy characteristics.

By first stopping, and then becoming aware of what is going on in the moment, we can discover what is interfering with the flow of our lives.

When we are born, we have a pure flow of energy that can quickly and easily become suppressed by our experiences. We can become like the faucet—clogged up with negative emotions. As a result, our thoughts and how we react to our experiences can cause us to lose our power. Then we form habitual patterns of reactions that pull us down and deplete our energy. We lose our connection to our soul. We lose our spiritual connection.

In a fascinating study, David R. Hawkins, M.D., Ph.D., spent over twenty years researching energy. His work involved millions of calibrations on thousands of test subjects of all ages and personality types, and from all walks of life. The study resulted in what he calls "The Map of Consciousness."[11] His research findings correlate with the conclusions reached by Nobelist Sir John Eccles—namely, that the brain acts as a receiving set for energy patterns residing in the mind itself, which exists as consciousness expressed in the form of thought. The following levels of energy are delegated to our emotions, from shame being the lowest at an energy level of 20 to peace being the highest at energy levels between 700 and 1000. This phenomenon is fully explained in Hawkins' book *Power vs. Force*.[12]

People below the 200 energy level tend to view themselves as powerless and to see themselves as victims. The world is seen as hopeless, sad, frightening or frustrating. The 200 energy level is

ENERGY LEVELS

Energy Levels	Emotional States	Energy Levels	Emotional State
20	Shame	250	Neutrality*
30	Guilt	310	Willingness
50	Apathy	350	Acceptance
75	Grief	400	Reason
100	Fear	500	Love
125	Desire	540	Joy
150	Anger	600	Peace
175	Pride	700–1000	Enlightenment**
200	Courage		

*Energy becomes positive at the neutral level because we have released our rigid positions at the lower levels. We have a sense of well-being. We can then move on to higher states of positive energy.

**Very few have entered the enlightened state, but those who have include great teachers, such as Moses, Buddha, Jesus and others.

the critical line that lies between the positive and negative influences of life. Sir John believes that we cannot have any meaningful human satisfaction until level 250, where some degree of self-confidence begins to emerge as a basis for positive life experiences. We take back our power at level 350.

Dr. Hawkins explains: "A 'high' is any state of consciousness above one's customary level of awareness. Therefore a person living in Fear, moving up to Anger (for instance, rioters in third-world ghettos) is a 'high.' Fear at least feels better than Despair, and Pride feels far better than Fear. Acceptance is much more comfortable than Courage, and Love makes any lower state comparatively unattractive. While Joy surpasses all lesser human emotions, ecstasy is a rarely felt emotion in a class by itself. The most sublime experience of all is a state of infinite peace so exquisite that it belies all attempts at description."[14]

I have been teaching about higher and lower energy thoughts for many years and have developed the following list:

Heavy, Lower Energy Thoughts Give Us a Heavy Heart

Anger	Judgments
Criticism	Negative Thinking
Fear	Pride
Guilt	Resentments
Greed	Self-Pity
Hate	Vengeance
Hypocrisy	Violence
Jealousy	Worry

Lighter, Higher Energy Thoughts Lighten Our Heart

Acceptance	Forgiveness
Appreciation	Generosity
Caring	Gratitude
Compassion	Joy
Creativity	Love
Faith	

Lower energy thoughts deplete our energy, reduce our ability to create a joyful, purposeful life and can cause poor health. If, for example, we are still carrying memories of earlier experiences that cause us shame, such as something we might have done as a child, it's time to talk about it and let it go. It is important that we examine what is making our hearts heavy.

We have all the energy states within us. Our practice is to recognize what we are feeling. We want to be aware without judgment. No feeling is good or bad, right or wrong—it just is.

If the feeling is pleasant, we want to prolong it and may engage in unhealthy actions to produce more pleasant feelings—for example, eating more food, having more sex, taking more drugs. These actions eventually lead to more pain.

If the feeling is unpleasant, we want to deny or push it away and again may engage in unhealthy actions to *mask* unpleasant feelings—again resorting to more food, sex, drugs, etc. These actions also eventually lead to more pain. An ideal state is when we don't want more or less of anything, but exactly what we have. It is in the acceptance of whatever we are feeling, without wishing it to be different, that the feeling is transformed. This is when we feel peace. This is the path to a light heart.

This book can begin to teach you how to lift your thoughts, bring joy into your days and find a purpose in your problems. We can train ourselves how to respond to each moment.

Lifting Our Thoughts

One beautiful way of lifting our thoughts to a higher level and thus raising our energy is to tap into a stored memory of joy, love or self-confidence. It takes only a few moments to make this happen.

Choose a time when you felt full of joy, love or self-confidence. You can choose another high-energy feeling if you wish. Close your eyes for a few minutes and picture how you felt at that time. Remember it with all your senses. As you breathe in and out, feel that experience all through your body.

The HeartMath Institute suggests that you place your hand over your heart during this exercise. After a few minutes, you can open your eyes. Practice this a few times to establish this memory within you. [14]

When you feel yourself filling with emotions like fear or anger, place your hand over your heart and watch how the negative feelings are replaced by feelings of joy and love. Remember that everything begins with a thought. A thought of fear leads to a feeling of fear. A thought of resentment leads to feelings of anger. When you become willing to get out of your head and come from your heart, your feelings change to loving feelings.

John Grassi, a teacher I had in graduate school, told me a wonderful story to illustrate this. At recess one day, two young students were getting ready to have a fight. A girl caught the attention of one of the boys and put her hand over her heart to remind him to come from his heart. In turn, that boy put his hand over his heart and stopped acting out his anger. The second boy saw this gesture, put *his* hand over his heart—and the fight was over.

It is such a simple exercise but it works every time we have the willingness to change.

Neale Donald Walsh writes, "The Highest Thought is the thought which contains joy. The Clearest Words are those that contain truth. The Grandest Feeling is that which you call love. Joy, truth and love. These three are interchangeable, and one always leads to the other. It matters not in which order they are placed."

Here are some questions you can ask yourself that will help

Guided Imagery for Healing

Here is a guided imagery that can help connect you with a higher frequency of energy for faster healing:

Imagine that you have a cord connected from the top of your head reaching up to all the energies of the universe. You can feel it vibrating. See a glow of light all around you, expanding wider and wider until all you see is light. Feel it vibrating as you sit in the center of all this energy. Feel your entire body alive and connected to this higher frequency. Feel yourself surrounded by love. In this powerful place, say to yourself, *All the energies of the universe are healing my body today.* See this manifesting. Know this is a reality.

Now give thanks for the manifestation of this affirmation.

you begin the Heart-Lightening Process. Take plenty of time and remember, there are no right or wrong answers:

- Can you see where you fit on the energy scale?
- What are you holding on to that keeps you from moving up to the next level?
- What are your obstacles to finding your higher purpose at this time of your life?
- What interferes with you knowing God?
- What blocks you from experiencing a light heart?
- What blocks you from reaching a higher state of consciousness?
- What are you holding on to that keeps you from feeling joy?

The Heart-Lightening Process
Step 3:

ACCEPT WHATEVER IS HAPPENING
WITHOUT JUDGMENT*

*When we accept ourselves in all
our weakness, flaws and failings, we can begin
to fulfill an even more challenging responsibility:
accepting the weakness, limitations, and*

---

*As explained in chapter one, only Step 1 and Step 2 are suggested to be done in order. The remainder of the steps are what I call "floating steps," and can be used in any order that works best for you.

BUSINESS REPLY MAIL

FIRST-CLASS MAIL PERMIT NO 45 DEERFIELD BEACH, FL

POSTAGE WILL BE PAID BY ADDRESSEE

HEALTH COMMUNICATIONS, INC.
3201 SW 15TH STREET
DEERFIELD BEACH FL 33442-9875

READER/CUSTOMER CARE SURVEY

BB4

We care about your opinions. Please take a moment to fill out this Reader Survey card and mail it back to us.
As a special "thank you" we'll send you exciting news about interesting books and a valuable Gift Certificate.

Please PRINT using ALL CAPS

First
Name _____ MI. ___ Last
Name _____

Address _____ City _____

ST ____ Zip _____ Email: _____

Phone # (____) _____ Fax # (____) _____

(1) Gender:
____ Female   ____ Male

(2) Age:
____ 12 or under   ____ 40-59
____ 13-19   ____ 60+
____ 20-39

(3) What attracts you most to a book?
(Please rank 1-4 in order of preference.)

	1	2	3	4
3) Title	○	○	○	○
4) Cover Design	○	○	○	○
5) Author	○	○	○	○
6) Content	○	○	○	○

(7) Where do you usually buy books?
Please fill in your top TWO choices.

1) ____ Bookstore
2) ____ Religious Bookstore
3) ____ Online
4) ____ Book Club/Mail Order
5) ____ Price Club (Costco, Sam's Club, etc.)
6) ____ Retail Store (Target, Wal-Mart, etc.)

Comments:
_____
_____
_____
_____
_____
_____
_____

mixed-up-ed-ness of those we love and respect.
Then and only then, it seems, do we become able
to accept the weakness, defects and shortcomings
of those we find it difficult to love.

—AUTHOR UNKNOWN

Accept whatever is going on completely, without any judgment. It is neither right nor wrong, good nor bad. It just is. Accept whatever is going on to the best of your ability—whether you have just won the lottery, lost your job or are in a noisy disagreement with your boss. This does not mean you don't feel the feelings, pleasurable or painful, but acceptance is key here.

Wouldn't it be wonderful if we could live like this, simply stop and be in the moment, without feelings of fear, anger or resentment? Without thinking that something is either right or wrong? Without judgments or prejudices? Wouldn't it be wonderful if we could simply accept whatever is going on in the moment and feel the peace that comes from such acceptance? Instead of beating ourselves up or praising ourselves by telling ourselves that something is good or bad, right or wrong, pleasant or unpleasant, we simply could say, "Oh, this is what it is." Then we could continue to go on with what we are doing without tension or stress.

Life happens. Hurricanes, earthquakes, rainbows and shooting stars all happen. As it's not possible for most of us to live in sunshine all the time, it's also not possible to live in joy all the time. On the other hand, if we find ourselves in a negative energy state, we need to look deeper to discover what is creating our heavy hearts.

It is not enough to acknowledge we have a characteristic we don't like. It's not enough to realize we are envious, for example, and then beat ourselves up with, "I shouldn't be this way. What's wrong with me?" The challenge comes in acknowledging and gently accepting that we are not perfect human beings. Once we see that we have within us every characteristic that exists, that we are capable of murder as well as of creating new life, we come again to a place of choice. We can agonize over this discovery, and we can feel shame and guilt over this uncomfortable knowledge, or we can be willing to accept all of who we are, our attributes as well as our imperfections. And, once we do that, we will know a freedom beyond words. We will no longer fear to look inside of ourselves. That which has blocked us from feeling love and compassion will begin to disappear. A weight will have been lifted from our shoulders, and we will be on our way to knowing joy. John-Roger with Paul Kaye wrote that acceptance has been called the first "law" of Spirit. "If you can accept what is, there is no conflict in life. There are no problems. There is no story. Accepting a situation, just as it is, closes the gap between what should be and what is."

There are very painful circumstances when it takes time to accept our reality. When someone we love dies, or we hear we have a life-threatening disease, for example, it takes time to accept this news. We might feel angry, despondent, depressed or a number of other emotions. If we can allow our feelings to be exactly what they are, accepting them for what they are without trying to change them or push them away, it helps us get through these difficult times.

We might vehemently declare, "This I will never accept!" If we can take this to the next step and accept what we judge as unacceptable, our pain can soften.

The very core of our suffering is when we will not accept reality as it is. We suffer when we want more and more of what feels good, adding to our good feelings. Or when we want to push away and deny that which feels terrible, we suffer. *The Course in Miracles* teaches that we are either coming from a place of love or coming from a place of fear. We either fear that we are not going to get what we want, or we fear that we will lose what we already have. Pere Caussade, an eighteenth-century Jesuit spiritual director counseled, "Only when we learn to put up with ourselves can we arrive at a place of interior peace."

There's a saying that goes, "Denial is not a river in Egypt." We often want to continue to do that which pleases us long after it pleases us. We hope that what we are doing will give us the high or the comfort or the fun or the fulfillment for which we so deeply hunger. We hope it will fill that empty place inside. Many years ago, when I had been going through a difficult time, my dear friend Mimi Kahn shared this quote with me, and it has been a great comfort: *Vous schver for menchen gring for God.* (What's hard for people is easy for God.) While I was writing this book, Mimi sent me the following story that she wrote, which speaks so very eloquently about acceptance and faith.

~

"I have never understood God, nor am I supposed to. But every now and then I seem to get a sliver of intuition about the way He works in my life.

"Several years ago, our youngest son fell ill during his second year in law school. It was diagnosed as a 'functional disorder'—in other words—a nervous breakdown. He did recover and the prognosis was good if he continued to take a small dose of one of the anti-hallucinogenic drugs.

"But, after a time, Scott felt the drug interfered with his analytical processes so he stopped taking it, unbeknownst to our family. As a result, Scott experienced a relapse, and we placed him in a fine mental health facility. Unfortunately, he was one tough cookie, and his doctors had a hard time reaching him.

"Dr. Lerman, the experienced psychiatrist who was in charge of his case, warned us that our son would probably not accept the sad facts of his condition and the subsequent treatment necessary, until 'he hit his bottom.'

"One day, Scott escaped from the hospital and came back to our home. The hospital had been in touch with us and warned us not to take Scott in or to help him in any way. No food, no clothing, no money and no shelter! It probably was one of the hardest things I'd ever done—refusing to give my own child even a drink of water.

"He remained in our backyard for a long time—and I watched him for hours through the kitchen window. When dusk fell, he left. There was nothing I could do about returning him to the hospital because his had been a voluntary commitment, and he needed to agree to it.

"*Later that night, a violent storm erupted. Rain fell in sheets and the thunder and lightning shook even our sturdy house. Waves of terror washed over me as I pictured my son— cold, wet and friendless—wandering about town.*

"*I began to pray with all the fervor I could command, 'Please, please, Lord, keep him safe tonight.' Over and over, I repeated this litany. Around midnight the phone rang. I picked it up but I almost couldn't speak because my heart had leaped into my throat. A man's voice asked if I were Mrs. Kahn and when I identified myself, he said, 'I'm Officer McCarthy at the Rockville Center Police Station. We have your son Scott here.'*

"'*Is he all right? Is he okay?'*

"'*Yes, he is, Ma'am. But we picked him up trying to break into the basement of the church. Now we're not planning to charge him . . .'*

"'*He's sick,' I blurted. 'He escaped from a mental hospital.'*

"'*Well, we understand that there's something wrong with him. Are you coming down to pick him up?'*

"*With all the strength I could muster up, I said, 'No, I'm not. What will you do with him?'*

"*The officer told me they would keep him overnight in a holding pen and, in the morning, transfer him to a county hos- pital for further evaluation.*

"*And I agreed.*

"*When I put down the phone and leaned back against the pillows, my thoughts whirled like the fragments of color in a kaleidoscope. My son, my young, brilliant attorney, was in a place that no one in our family had* ever *been, in a jail.*

"*But when the pieces settled and I saw the design—I real- ized that God had answered my prayers. I hadn't asked that*

*Scott be found safe in the Plaza Hotel—I had only entreated
that he be found safe.*

"And for that night he was. And I thanked my God."

—

We often want what we want when we want it. We can't stand
to be in that "place of not knowing," that place that only patience
and faith and trust can fill. And yet when we dwell on what we
don't know, stamping our feet and demanding unattainable answers,
it is impossible to live with a light heart. It is impossible to come
from a place of love.

We also create stories about what happens to make us feel
better. Christine Feldman told a wonderful story in her book *The
Buddhist Path to Simplicity*. She wrote about how we can walk out of
doors and stub our toe on a stone. "The simple truth of the moment
is the toe and the stone, the meeting and the sensation. Instead we
might carry on: 'My toe!' 'Which fool put that stone there?' 'Why
do these things happen to me?' This brings so much more into the
moment and pulls us down and makes the situation worse. If we
would just come from the place of simple acceptance, simply seeing
'the toe' and 'the stone' without the story, we would find peace."

Acceptance is an anecdote for judgment, perfection and resentments. We can learn to let go of being judgmental by practicing
acceptance. We can learn to let go of perfectionism by the practice
of acceptance. We can learn to let go of anger and resentments by
the practice of acceptance.

For example, I had an interesting discussion in a recent meditation class about forgiveness. One meditator wondered if forgiveness is really necessary. We began to explore this idea. If we completely accept whatever is, whether it is a person or situation, then forgiveness is not necessary. On the other hand, if we are holding on to resentments from the past or if we feel guilty about something we have done, then we must forgive ourselves and others.

As we learn to live light as a feather, acceptance becomes a very important characteristic for us to practice. We learn to see clearly what can or cannot be done in the moment. Through prayer we can learn what is God's will and what is our will. And through prayer we can turn over that which seems impossible and trust that God will see us through it.

LETTING GO AFFIRMATION

*And could you keep your heart in wonder
at the daily miracles of your life, your pain would
not seem less wondrous than your joy.*

—Kahlil Gibran

Our thoughts can give us negative, fearful and angry messages, but our hearts always give us love. When we come from our hearts, we feel lighter. We are connected to God, to our truth. The burdens from our self-talk disappear.

Learning to make decisions from our hearts can be a big change for us. We've been taught to be logical and practical. But there are times when our mind tells us one thing and our hearts tell us something else. There are times when we must follow our inner voices and let our hearts be in charge.

We only have this present moment. We can't bring it back. If we make the most of it, follow the guidance of our hearts, we bring lightness to the moment and to each succeeding moment.

*Today I am taking time to put my hand
on my heart and let the love and joy that I feel
flow through me and on to everyone
that is on my path.*

CHAPTER

4

Letting Go of
Negative Blocks

Prayers to Sophia

Transforming Presence,
layers and layers of my false self
keep being stripped away from me.
I walk with caterpillar feet,
knowing that the skin must be shed
time and again
before I find my butterfly wings.

I look at the old discarded peelings
of the person I thought I was
with some dismay and sadness,
but also with some relief and joy.

With every lifted layer, I feel lighter,
With every painful peeling, I am freer,
With every discarded skin, I stretch deeper,
With every sloughed off segment, I grow wiser.

Keep teaching me, Freedom Bringer,
that it is never too late
to embrace the changes
that lead to my truest self.
Keep nudging me away from confining security
when I cling too tightly to what needs to go.

Continue to attune my spirit to your song
of ongoing transformation.
Remind me daily that I will always have
another layer that needs to be shed.

—Joyce Rupp, *Peeling Off Another Layer*

It's the heart that lets go,
the fingers just follow.

—African Proverb

J oy exists in our hearts. Love exists in our hearts. When we feel love, we feel joy. Our purpose is, as it says in *A Course in Miracles,* removing the blocks to our natural inheritance, which is the awareness of love's presence. Our goal is to find out who we really are, once we let go of all our blocks.

When our hearts are filled with hate, anger, greed or any of the negative emotions that diminish our energy, we can't feel joy. When we are grasping, wanting or impatient, when we want more and more and there is never enough, we can't feel peace. When we hang on to our suffering with great tenacity, stuck in destructive patterns such as: "This I will never forget," or "He doesn't deserve my forgiveness," we live with low energy and a heavy heart. Our immune system becomes threatened, leading to a variety of diseases.

Some of us still carry the suffering from our childhoods, resentments from early disappointments, blaming parents or caretakers for the heaviness we feel in our hearts or for the fact that we don't feel at all. If we are filled with anger, resentment and self-pity, among other burdens of the heart, we continue to attract more of the same to us because we experience the world in a negative way. Some of us will die never knowing that we could have transcended our suffering and pain and lived with more joy and purpose.

We have to be willing to shine a light in our hearts and explore all that is blocking us, looking without fear, guilt and shame—just looking, knowing that enlightenment is waiting for us at the end of our search. With each discovery that we make, our hearts become lighter and we are farther along on our path to living light as a feather.

The key to your search is honesty. Whenever you discover a block, simply notice it, without judgment. If your immediate reaction is to blame someone or something, or you notice a resentment or a feeling of shame, *stop*. Take a deep breath. First get in touch with the feelings that accompany your reaction, and then accept it. Something deeper lies under this reaction. You will find that we either come from a place of love or from a place of fear. You will find that under jealousy, anger, hate, criticism and other emotions lies fear. And it's always fear of losing something we already have or fear that we will not get what we want. When we have fear, we are coming from a place of self-centeredness. As we let go, we will be moving into a place of other-centeredness.

The more you practice the Heart-Lightening Process, the more blocks you will discover and the more you will experience the joy of watching them take up a smaller and smaller space in your heart. And as they shrink, more joy will enter.

In this chapter I have highlighted some of the emotions and patterns that fill us with heavy hearts.

Addictions

Because gratification of a desire leads
to the temporary stilling of the mind and the
experience of the peaceful, joyful self, it's no wonder
that we get hooked on thinking that happiness
comes from the satisfaction of desires.

—JOAN BORYSENKO

Material possessions, such as houses, cars and jewelry, make us feel good for the moment. But we have a deeper longing inside, a spiritual longing that no person or thing can satisfy. Some of us turn to alcohol or drugs, excitement, sex, or dozens of other experiences to fill this emptiness. They, too, bring some satisfaction, but it is only temporary, and they themselves can become a great problem and lead to addictions. Soon we want more and more of what makes us feel good, and we want to push away our pain and discomfort. Eventually we have no choice and we need help to let go.

I sometimes have book signings that are very well attended, where people respond enthusiastically to my talk and end up buying many books. I feel energized, affirmed, successful and grateful. And then there are other times when only a few people show up. These occasions could be depressing if I let them be. Never knowing which will happen, I began saying a prayer before each signing: "Please help me be there for why You want me to be there." From that time on, there has never been a depressing signing. There is always someone there who has a question or a problem. And whether or not anyone buys a book, there is always a positive connection.

There was one special book signing I'll never forget. It was just a few days before Christmas, and I was a little tired, having already traveled many miles for many days, sometimes doing up to three book signings a day. This was the last one for the season. As I drove to the bookstore, I remembered to say my prayer.

I was pleased to see all my books placed on a table near the entrance with a sign and a chair. Just a few minutes after I sat down, a small, very sweet-looking woman with white hair came slowly up to me, carrying two each of all my books in her arms. She bent down and whispered in my ear. "I am seventy-five years old, and I've been drinking every day for forty years, and I haven't been able to stop." Shivers went through me. I knew this was why I was there that day. We talked for a long time. I asked her if she believed in God, and she said she did. I then suggested that she ask for help to have God remove the desire to drink. I shared some of my story with her and told her about a meeting I go to on Sunday mornings, which other people with similar issues attend to talk about them. She hesitated and said she probably couldn't go because she attended church on Sundays.

That was on a Tuesday. I was busy that week and forgot about our encounter, but the next Sunday morning as I was getting a cup of tea at the meeting that I had suggested she attend, I felt a tap on my shoulder. I turned around and was amazed to see the woman from the bookstore. My eyes filled with tears. She told me she had not had a drink since the previous Tuesday.

Kathy was her name, and her best friend came with her for support. They were there again almost every Sunday for a year. Kathy was painfully shy and was petrified that she would have to speak at a meeting someday. I assured her she wouldn't have to, so she continued to attend these Sunday meetings.

As I learned later, Kathy had also suffered from depression most of her life. Alcohol was the only thing that seemed to relieve her for a period of time, so she had been using it to self-medicate. When she stopped drinking, there were times when her depression was very deep, but Kathy hung in there, having her antidepressants adjusted by her doctor, as needed. She also came to my meditation classes, with the hope that they would help, and worked with affirmations to free her from her depression. In time the miracle happened, and her depression lifted.

I had the honor of helping her celebrate her first-year anniversary without a drink the December after we met. Friends and family came to our meeting to celebrate with her. Kathy, in spite of her painful shyness, was able to speak and thank everyone for supporting her through that wonderful year.

Then the unthinkable happened. I received an e-mail from her close friend with the devastating news that Kathy had breast cancer. I immediately called her and was surprised to find she was bright and cheerful. "If I could get through a year without drinking and have my depression lifted, I can get through anything!" she said. And she did. She went through surgery and chemotherapy and is doing fine. In fact, that year she fulfilled a lifetime desire to go to Medjugorje in Bosnia. She had always been afraid to make long-term plans or to travel because her depressions could force her to bed, and she never knew when she would have them, but she made her trip overseas and had a wonderful time.

~~~

Anger and Fear

We are only as big as the smallest thing that makes us angry.

—Author Unknown

The reason that I am placing anger and fear together is that I believe they go hand in hand. Fear is usually the motivator underneath anger. We are angry because we are afraid. When we are fearful, we usually lash out at someone else or direct the anger at ourselves. Anger turned inward leads to depression.

Both anger and fear are natural, God-given, even protective emotions. They are energizing, but they must be expressed in a healthy way. If not, they lie heavily in our hearts, as hard as a rock, blocking out our natural feelings of love and compassion. It's interesting to note that the word anger is only one letter short of danger.

Bill Wilson, cofounder of Alcoholics Anonymous wrote, "The achievement of freedom from fear is a lifetime undertaking, one that can never be wholly completed. When under heavy attack, acute illness, or in other conditions of serious insecurity, we shall all react to this emotion—well or badly, as the case may be. Only the self-deceived will claim perfect freedom from fear."[1] He went on to say that the basic antidote to fear is a spiritual awakening.[2]

I think anger is one of the most difficult emotions to understand—more precisely, knowing how one should deal with anger is most difficult.

Anger hurts us more than the person with whom we are angry. Thich Nhat Hanh has said that when we are angry at someone, it is like holding a burning coal in our hand, ready to throw it at the person with whom we are angry, only to find that it burns us first!

I can still picture the time I ran out of my house when I was a child to get away from my father because he had pulled off his belt and threatened to beat me with it. I was around eight or nine. I ran down our block, into someone's backyard, climbed over a fence and hid. He threatened me often, but he never once actually hit me with his belt, and only once did he hit me with his hand. Even so, the fear stayed with me long into my adulthood.

When my father was angry, his face would become red, and it looked as if he would explode. Sometimes I would run into my room and lock the door when he yelled and threatened me. He would bang on the door, ordering me to open it, which I didn't dare to do as I was afraid of being hit. He would yell, "No allowance for you!" My mother would come to the door and beg me to open it. "If you don't open the door your father will have a heart attack," she would plead. What a choice. Be hit or be responsible for my father's death. The next morning I would find a dollar bill slipped under my door to soothe his guilt. He thought that made everything all right.

He and I argued all the time. When I left for college I vowed I would stop arguing with him. What I did, of course, was stuff my feelings. I didn't know that was what I was doing at the time. I thought I had learned to stop being angry. Little did I know then that suppressing anger can turn to rage or depression, and that suppressing any emotions is unhealthy mentally, physically and spiritually.

Many years later I still carried the fear of my father's threat of pain, even though he did hit me only once, as I recall. It took me years to be able to stand up to him without fear. One time I remember writing a note to him, telling him I did not want him to drive my children when he had been drinking. He wrote back, "DON'T YOU EVER TALK TO ME LIKE THAT AGAIN." Still yelling!

Ambrose Redmoon wrote that courage is not the absence of fear, but rather the judgment that something else is more important than fear. That time came again for me two days before my mother died. Unbeknownst to my father, my mother had put away $5,000 into a savings account because her intention was to leave $1,000 to each of her five grandchildren. My father somehow found out about the money, went to the bank, got a signature card from them and brought it to the hospital. My mother was heavily medicated for the pain of her stomach cancer, so he was able to convince her to sign it.

When my brother called to see how our mother was, I told him about the card. He told me I had to get the card and rip it up. Mustering all the strength I had, I casually asked my father to see the card and then proceeded to rip it up. He was furious. His face grew an angry red. I quickly kissed my mother goodnight and rushed to the elevator. While waiting for it to arrive, my father stood before me, a seventy-five-year-old man, veins bulging from his neck, with arms raised over his head and shaking his fist at me. "I should hit you right now!" he threatened. I looked at him calmly and got into the elevator.

It was finally over. It was hard for me to believe that I had held on to this fear for so long. I was thirty-eight years old, married, the mother of three children, and until that moment, I was still afraid of my father. Now I was finally free of my fear, but it took many years for me to become free of the resentments I held against him.

If we look deeply into our anger, we can often find that the true feeling beneath it is almost always fear. We are either afraid of losing something we already have or we fear not getting something we want. Deepak Chopra has said, "If you look under your depression, you'll find anger. Look under your anger, and you'll find sadness. And under sadness is the root of it all, what's really masquerading all the while—fear." My father was furious at me because my actions caused him to lose $5,000. I was furious at him because I was afraid he would keep my mother from having her last wishes honored—leaving her hard-earned money to her grandchildren.

The "Big Book" of Alcoholics Anonymous tells us that there is no such thing as justifiable anger. My interpretation of that is that we cannot afford to hold on to anger. The HeartMath Institute explains that "physiologically, it simply doesn't matter whether the anger is justified or not. The body doesn't make moral judgments about feelings; it just responds accordingly."[3] As you examine your anger and get to the bottom of it, be gentle with yourself when you discover that the root of your anger is fear. Fear is simply another natural emotion. Remember, the body doesn't make moral judgments about feelings, and we shouldn't either.

One way out of anger is through it and then on to acceptance and forgiveness. You will see more on forgiveness in chapter five.

All anger isn't destructive. Anger can be a problem that we turn into a purpose by taking positive action steps. On a personal level, anger can be a great motivator to leave a unsatisfactory job or unhappy relationship. On a larger scale, anger at homelessness, poverty, child labor and prejudice, to name a few injustices, have resulted in healthy social change. Let's hope this continues so we can see an end to war!

Guilt and Shame

Reexamine all you have been told....
Dismiss what insults your Soul.

—WALT WHITMAN

Most of us are taught right from wrong when we are very young. But just because we learn not to lie, steal or hurt another person, it does not mean we are always going to honor these rules. A stolen candy bar here, a little white lie there, can sometimes sit as guiltily on our conscience as a larger crime. It's amazing how the smallest transgression pops up to disturb us when we begin our spiritual journey. Actions we have taken that we know are wrong cause guilt.

Shame, on the other hand, is something we internalize. Until we have developed a strong sense of self, that self is a reflection of the opinions of others. For example, if we have been told that we will never amount to anything, we accept that as truth until we learn that was simply someone else's opinion.

Some messages that we hear as children remain deeply buried in our subconscious and can become heavy burdens that we carry with us in our hearts. Because they are invisible, we often do not know they are there. Instead we react to each new situation as if we were still children. The triggers set within these messages by the adults and peers in our childhood are so heavy they can pull us down, keeping us locked in a repetitive pattern of behavior that blocks our progress throughout our lives.

For example, when I was around six or seven years old, I received a pair of shiny new roller skates for my birthday. They had crimson metal wheels, so bright and pretty—I loved them! I remember we had a cement patio-like porch with a wrought iron railing in the front of our house, and I couldn't wait to put them on and try them out there.

It was a cool fall day, perfect for skating. I went round and round in big circles, deep into the thrill of the experience, concentrating with everything I had to keep from falling. I was wobbly at first but I was upright! A tapping noise brought me back to my surroundings. My mom and dad were watching me from the living room window. They motioned for me to come inside.

"We thought you would love your skates," my mother said, accusingly, with obvious disappointment.

"I do!" I remember saying with enthusiasm to reassure her.

"But you're not smiling," she said, convinced that I wasn't happy with their gift.

I had been feeling so good about myself, concentrating so hard, so proud that I wasn't falling and that I was learning so quickly. But there was that message again, the message that had been planted that something was wrong with me. I hadn't "enjoyed" myself the "right" way. I didn't live up to my parent's expectations of what was happy. They didn't see what I was feeling and concluded from their perspective that I wasn't happy. I felt such disappointment that I hadn't pleased them. I felt rejected.

My parents didn't understand me. I know today that they only wanted me to be happy. But it had to be what they thought happiness was. I didn't bubble with enthusiasm and smile all the time, because I had a serious, contemplative nature.

Over the years I received more messages about my not smiling enough. My mother told me I had such a pretty smile. "Why don't you use it more often?" she would ask. That made me even more self-conscious about my smile. I remember going to the mirror and practicing smiling. When I saw my face in the mirror, I noticed a line above my lip that became indented when I smiled and I remember thinking that my smile wasn't very pretty at all.

From roller skating on my front porch when I was eight, to a time in my late thirties, the message stayed with me, creating self-consciousness and becoming a block to my self-esteem. Then I finally began my spiritual journey and learned how to remove old messages that weren't mine in the first place.

For many years Patti was filled with both shame and guilt, as her story beautifully illustrates.

⌒

Patti was the third daughter of four children, and she absolutely adored her father. She always wanted to please him and did whatever she could to impress him.

By the time she was in the eighth grade, she began having feelings for other girls and became extremely uncomfortable about who she was. She was sure her father would be furious if he ever found out as he was an extremely prejudiced person. So she covered up her feelings by becoming the joker who laughed a lot and made others laugh as well. Later, she began drinking to make herself feel better. By the time she was in her late teens, Patti began having one-night stands with men, trying to change who she was.

Patti married at twenty-one and had a son. For the eleven years she and her husband were married, they drank, partied and played sports together. On the outside it looked as if they were happy and well matched.

Because she had held so much of her feelings in all her life, Patti began developing an anxiety disorder that mutated into agoraphobia. Her fears grew until she couldn't even leave the house to go to the grocery store. She couldn't drive her car. Her drinking picked up as well, so her doctor was reluctant to put her on medication. Unable to manage Patti's pain, her husband finally left her.

Desperate for relief, Patti finally entered a recovery program and found a God of her understanding. Scared to death, she also found the courage to tell someone about her feelings for women. "Big deal," was the reply, and Patti finally began feeling some relief. She asked for help from God with the prayer: "If I am gay, if this is who I am, please help me to accept it."

"I had been too frightened to accept the truth about myself," Patti later said. "Why would anyone else?"

Soon she took the next gigantic step—she told her family. It was the scariest thing Patti had ever done. All but one distant cousin accepted her completely. Since she has become honest with who she is, life has really changed for her. She has a wonderful new relationship and her fears have almost all gone away.

Notice the messages that run your life. Jot them down as you hear them. We need to open our hearts to messages such as these and realize once and for all they aren't true. We must let them go; as we do, our hearts will be on the path to becoming as light as a feather.

As you practice mindfulness you will become aware of other patterns and habitual behaviors that lead to unhappiness and pain. Discover the ones that fill you with shame. Are you experiencing repeated difficulties in your relationships? Do you have a problem holding on to money or a job? Does it appear that people are always taking advantage of you? Are you often sick or lethargic? Ask yourself these and other questions and watch carefully what you think and how you act. Remember not to judge yourself, but simply note and accept all that you discover. This is your opportunity to let go and let God.

By following the Heart-Lightening Process, we can stop, see what is weighing so heavily on our conscience, accept it and take an action step to let it go. Expressing how we are feeling to a trusted friend, therapist, sponsor or clergy is the beginning of letting go. Making amends and then forgiving ourselves might follow. You'll find out more about this in chapter five.

Grief

Let go of your expectations.
The universe will do what it will.
Sometimes your dreams will come true.
Sometimes they won't. Sometimes when you
let go of a broken dream, another
one gently takes its place.

—MELODY BEATTIE

Usually we think of grief as something we feel when a person or pet we love dies. Yet there are many other losses that require us to take time to grieve. When we lose a job, a relationship, a business or a lifestyle, it takes time to get over the feelings of emptiness and loss. We need to honor the feelings that we experience. When we let go of habits and addictions, there is an empty space. Something is missing and it hurts. Letting go of alcohol, drugs, smoking, gambling, overeating and other addictions all leave an empty space, a gap in our lives. In time, this gap will be filled with positive feelings. But it is healthy to feel their loss. We have used many diversions to block feelings of pain, inadequacy and fear. The Heart-Lightening Process teaches us new ways to deal with the unpleasant feelings that come up in the natural course of life.

Elizabeth Kübler-Ross teaches that grief, shame and guilt are not very far removed from feelings of anger and rage. Grief has its own stages that one must go through, as Kübler-Ross points out in her groundbreaking book *On Death and Dying*. The five stages are: denial and isolation; anger; bargaining; depression and, finally, acceptance.

When we don't experience the pain of our loss, it stays stuck in our hearts, needing to be expressed, before we can heal.

Let your grief take its own natural course. No one is exactly the same as anyone else, and there is no way of determining how long it will take to move on with your life. The feelings from some losses may never go away entirely, but we learn to cope with them and fit them into our lives in a healthy way. Planting a tree or making a donation in the name of the person who died are two of many healthy ways we can deal with our grief. Having a special ceremony on the anniversary of the death of a loved one, or on their birthday, is another way.

My son, Bob, loved fried clams, so each year we go out for fried clams in honor of his birthday to celebrate his life. Rituals such as these are another healthy way to stay connected with someone we love who has passed away.

Sarah's story is a wonderful example of how rituals also help in healing our grief.

⌒

There were two things that made Michele happy. One was motorcycling, no matter how much pain she felt. And the other was fishing. She would fish for hours and hours, no matter how much pain she was in. For the twelve years they were together, Sarah and Michele spent a week or two in Vermont every year. The two women would go out on the lake at sunrise while Michele fished and Sarah read. After a few hours, Sarah would go back to shore, and Michele would stay out fishing. So when Michele—who had been HIV positive since before they met—died, Sarah decided to spread her ashes in Vermont where they had vacationed for years.

Many of their friends joined together for the ceremony. When the sun rose, they gathered together and went out on the lake in a few boats to spread Michele's ashes. They sat and told stories and laughed and cried together. That evening they sat outside thinking about Michele, and a bright star appeared. Someone said, "Look! There's the first star!" And someone else said, "That's no star. That's Michele!"

A healing ritual was created. Every night, from that time on, Sarah looks up at the first star and says, "Hi, Michele. How are you doing?"

"Every time I see that star, I see Michele grin," said Sarah. "This gives me healing and great joy." Michele was a very loving person and had many friends. Many struggled with her death. Sarah has told them the story of the first star, and many of them are following the same ritual, saying, "Hi, Michele," to her each night.

⌒

Judgments and Opinions

Everything that irritates
us about others can lead us to an
understanding of ourselves.

—CARL JUNG

Being judgmental keeps us separated from others. When we feel better than or less than others, we cut ourselves off. What we often don't realize is that our judgments are only a result of our thinking. Very often, they are even a result of someone else's thinking! We hold on to opinions and judgments taught to us from early childhood, taking them on as if they were our own. We decide this is right or wrong, that is good or bad.

Author Stephen Covey writes, "Look at the weaknesses of others with compassion, not accusation. It's not what they're not doing or should be doing that's the issue. The issue is your own chosen response to the situation and what you should be doing. If you start to think the problem is 'out there,' stop yourself; that thought is the problem."

I had a wonderful example of this many years ago when Sandy Bierig, then the codirector of Serenity House in Natick, Massachusetts, started a unique program in MCI Framingham, a women's prison. Until that time, there wasn't an in-house program that directly dealt with addiction inside a women's prison. As it turned out, over ninety percent of the women in prison were there because of alcohol- or drug-related crimes. They had either committed a crime to acquire drugs or they had committed a crime while high on substances.

I was just learning to meditate then, but Sandy saw the tremendous difference it was making in my life. She invited me to come up to the prison once a week to teach meditation to some of the women in her program. Relatively new to meditation, I was not sure if I was qualified to do this. I asked permission from my own teacher, Larry Rosenberg, founder of the Cambridge Insight Meditation Society in Cambridge, Massachusetts. His answer was no, and I was actually not surprised. However, Larry took me aside at the end of the class the following week and said, "I've changed my mind. Go ahead and teach meditation to the women in prison. I was only afraid it could do you harm. If you go in there with high expectations and find that the women do not take to it, you might become disappointed and discouraged. You can't do any harm to them. They'll either be drawn to it or not."

With that encouragement, I filled out the necessary paperwork for clearance to enter the prison. When the approval finally came, I nervously drove over to conduct my first class. Even though I had been forewarned, I was very ill at ease when they put me through their search and had me lock up my wrist watch, credit cards, money and license. At last I walked through a heavy iron gate, shivering as it slammed shut behind me.

Once inside, I found myself sitting before a dozen or so women, most with their arms crossed, some tapping their feet with impatience and all with a look of "Show me! I know this isn't going to work. What kind of foolishness are you going to tell us?" That was how I interpreted their looks, anyway. They all seemed hard to me. One was in for murder. The others for breaking and entering, drinking and driving, or stealing. This was not a population I was comfortable with in those days. I was sure I would never reach them. They were tough and very different from me, I thought. How could they possibly relate to me?

When I began my first lesson, only a few women participated. The others looked up at the ceiling. Some whispered to each other, and some just glared at me. A few women stretched out in their chairs, yawned and closed their eyes. I remained nervous. My fearful thoughts had become the reality of the experience. It went on for a few weeks like this while I prayed that I could be a better teacher. I had shared with them from the beginning that I, too, was a recovering alcoholic, hoping that would help bridge the gap between their experiences and mine. Only a few had responded. I understood what my teacher had feared, but I kept praying.

Around the third week something happened. I felt different as I looked out at the women in orange jumpsuits or jeans with plain tops. I suddenly got it. I knew in that moment that we were exactly the same, that I could be sitting right where they were in one split second if I had picked up one more drink. I suddenly knew that nothing more than luck had kept me from killing someone with my car when I drove in a blackout. Lucky to have creative ability, I had started my own business while in college. I didn't have to steal to satisfy my own addiction. I was no better, no smarter and no more deserving to be free and able to walk out of the prison at the end of the sessions. One more drink could have put me behind bars, too. We were separated by something as small as one liquid ounce of alcohol or one pill.

All my tension and anxiety disappeared. I remember feeling softer. I had been holding myself so tightly that my jaw ached. Now I felt warm and I smiled as I shared this insight with the group. From then on it was a joy coming into the prison. The wall that my ego had erected by telling me that I was better and smarter disappeared. I'm not saying that all the women responded in a positive way, but enough did to make it a very satisfying, fulfilling experience. What a joy to see their faces soften and relax enough to learn a new technique with which they could find inner peace. For me, that was the beginning of many years of teaching meditation to many different people all over the country.

Feeling this deep connection to people who were, I thought, so very different from me was a major breakthrough. I had always felt better than or not as good as others. My early memories of connectedness went back to people just like me.

Oh, if we could just learn to be in the moment, be here and be mindful, without taking our past with us, without deciding what is right or wrong for us or someone else, according to our past thinking.

A car cuts in front of us and we might yell, "Jerk!" A person from another country wears something we have not seen before, and we might think it strange, rather than just different.

I remember sitting in a doctor's waiting room suddenly aware that my mind had scanned, one by one, all those in the room with me and, yes, judged them all.

Where do these thoughts even come from—the words that flash instantly into our minds and sometimes as quickly out of our mouths before we can stop them from doing harm? They seem to come naturally. Are we born with them? Are we born with a program that immediately tells our mouths to react to what our eyes see and our ears hear? Is a button pushed in our brain so our mouth says things like: "She's too fat . . .What a beautiful color that blouse is . . . He's so negative . . . She's too sweet to be real."

Our likes and our dislikes are always with us. Our brains are constantly in motion until we can learn to be mindful. Until we can say, "Stop! No more!" But why should we bother to stop? Why not just let our minds go wherever they want to go? What is the harm?

One day I had a wonderful moment of enlightenment. I had just polished my sneakers, something I might have done only two or three times in my life before, and then went to a meeting. I remember looking across the room and seeing a young man with dirty sneakers. *What a slob!* I heard myself think. I had a sudden flash, like lightning, in that moment. I saw what I had done. I saw my judgmental mind in action, and I actually embarrassed myself.

The death of my son, Bob, brought more lessons. Just a few days after he died, I remember walking from my car to a store. I was aware of how empty I felt. I was aware of my complete lack of energy, amazed that I could even put one foot in front of the other. I knew I couldn't even muster a smile. And I remember thinking to myself, *I hope you'll never judge another human being who doesn't respond to your smile, your hello. Maybe they, too, just lost someone dear or heard bad news or lost a job.*

Within weeks of my "smile insight," I was asked to read a schedule at a meeting. Again I remember feeling dull, depressed—certainly not enthusiastic. I didn't want to be up there at that microphone, but I did it for a friend who couldn't be there. And then I heard a man in the second row say to the person next to him, "If she can't put more enthusiasm into what she is saying, why does she even bother?" And I remember thinking, *If he only knew.*

If I had carried a cane in my hand or wore a bandage on my forehead, I would have had doors opened for me and smiles of sympathy. But the bruises in my heart were invisible. We don't know for sure what anyone is feeling at any given time.

Negative judgments, like old opinions, keep us from being in the moment and keep us from really experiencing what is going on. By coming from a place of compassion rather than judgment, as is so beautifully expressed in the next verse, we would feel so much more relaxed, peaceful and lighter!

If I Had Known

If I had known what troubles you were bearing,
What griefs were in the silence of your face,
I would have been more gentle and more caring,
And tried to give you gladness for a space.
I would have brought more warmth into the place—
If I had known.
If I had known what thoughts despairing drew you—
Why do we never understand?

I would have lent a little friendship to you,
And slipped my hand within your lonely hand,
And made your stay more pleasant in the land,
If I had known.

—Author Unknown

Sometimes we judge or compare to make ourselves feel good. "His sneakers are so dirty. Look at mine! I took time to clean mine!" or "Look at the way that guy is dressed. He's wearing cut-off shorts and sneakers to this nice restaurant."

Author and teacher Charlotte Joko Beck suggests that we look at how our body responds to judgment. She writes, ". . . whenever we judge, our body tightens up. Behind the judgment is a self-centered thought that produces tension in our body. Over time the tension is harmful to us, and indirectly harmful to others. Not only is the tension harmful, the judgments we express about others (and ourselves) are harmful, too."[4]

There is an old Indian saying that goes, "Never judge anyone until you have walked a mile in their moccasins."

We often judge from pure habit. It's how our minds work until we stop and hear ourselves. We learn it from our parents, peers, teachers, or relatives.

The Dalai Lama advises that happiness begins "with developing an understanding of the truest sources of happiness and setting our priorities in life based on the cultivation of those sources. It involves an inner discipline, a gradual process of rooting out destructive mental states and replacing them with positive, constructive states of mind such as kindness, tolerance, and forgiveness."[5]

This is not to say that there isn't a positive place for judgments. The dictionary also refers to judgments as "the ability to judge wisely; discernment; discrimination." This involves choice. Where would we be if we did not have the ability to choose from right and wrong, make healthy decisions about the food we eat, the friends in our lives, the partners we choose, the jobs we take, etc?

So, we can add negative judgments and opinions to the column of destructive mental states that drain our energy and block our hearts from feeling connected to the person we are judging.

Life's Struggles

We're not really in partnership with God without letting go, so we never really receive the gifts. Without letting go, the feeling of God's Presence is intermittent. The sense of God's guidance is occasional. And the change that we deeply want never gets a chance to blossom.

—MARY MANIN MORRISSEY

There is a story told that when Ralph Waldo Emerson's library of precious books was on fire, Louisa May Alcott tried to console him. The great philosopher said to her, "Yes, yes, Louisa, they're all gone. But let's enjoy the blaze now." Now, that's really letting go and living in the present moment!

There are so many things we have to let go of to become lighter. Some are easier than others. As we grow spiritually, we become clearer on what sits heavily in our hearts, blocking us from joy. As we grow in our ability to live mindfully—being present to what we can change and what we have to accept—our willingness to let go grows. It is easy to see the value of letting go of some things, such as anger and resentment, impatience and procrastination. Experience teaches us that when the decision is made, for example, to let go of habits or people that are harmful or negative in our lives, relief often comes quickly. Other times the pain of letting go can be very strong. Or we let go as we see the need for it. Sometimes we let go when the pain of holding on is greater than the pain of letting go. And sometimes we let go because it is the right thing to do, even though it appears to cause us more pain than joy.

Letting go of an unhealthy marriage is one example. Putting a parent in a nursing home is another. Buddha tells us that we need to let go of our expectations for they cause us to suffer. And yet, we suffer when we let go of someone or something that we love. Pride tells us we can make this situation work. Reality, when we acknowledge it, tells us that the situation is beyond our ability to handle.

We can stay locked in that place of trying to ignore the truth, and remain unable to move forward, or we can pray for the willingness to let go. Such is the challenge that Nancy faced.

"I tell myself that I can learn from this," says Nancy, who finally arrived at the truth that she must find a nursing home for her mother. "It's horrible that it is happening, but I know there is a lesson here, and I can learn from it. My heart is so much lighter when I approach things that way."

Nancy had struggled for years trying to take care of her mother and finally accepted that it wasn't her job. Her eighty-four-year-old mother's perspective is becoming so narrow that she can't connect with anything outside of herself. Nancy watches her mother and sees that as soon as she wakes up, life becomes all about her and her own bodily functions. Nancy realizes that her mother has always been basically self-centered, and she sees that now her mother's old behaviors are becoming magnified as she experiences increasing cognitive loss and smaller horizons.

Nancy also sees that some people in the nursing home she chose for her mother are interested in things other than themselves. They might ask the nurse her name, or whether she has a family, or what she thinks about the latest terrorist attack. Her mother doesn't think about anything other than that she can't find her moisturizer.

Nancy is observing and learning how people function as they grow older. Some withdraw into a very small world, like her mother. Others stay open and participate in the world around them. Nancy knows she will have a choice when it comes her turn to be cared for at the end of her life.

Nancy's original vision had been that her mother would come to live with her, and she would take care of her until she died. "I thought I'd be able to handle it. I thought I'd be able to maintain my own lifestyle and handle caring for my mother, too." However, it became too stressful for both of them when her mother's health began to fail, and she became almost totally unable to get around on her own.

The doctor suggested that they look into alternative care. The physical therapist said that they should look into alternative care. The visiting nurse suggested that they look into alternative care. Only when she had to assist her mother to the bathroom four or five times a night, when she was so exhausted and so stressed that she could barely function, did Nancy finally become open to the idea.

Once the decision was made, her mother was in agreement. Nancy knew she would agree because she had always been very compliant. At that point, her mother also started becoming more and more detached from the world around her and all the people in it.

The biggest problem they had was with the doctor. Her mother had to be put in the hospital for evaluation first, before she could be admitted to a nursing home. As Murphy's Law would have it, when Nancy decided that it was time for her mother to go, her mother was suddenly, if briefly, feeling a little better. Because of this, the doctor decided she didn't need the hospital as much that week. "She was ready last week," the doctor said. "Yes," responded Nancy, "but I wasn't ready last week. I'm ready this week."

Nancy had many feelings to process with this huge decision. The biggest disappointment was accepting she would not be able to take care of her mother herself. She had years and years of old tapes that told her she was supposed to take care of her. Now, a healthier Nancy took over, and she finally learned that it wasn't her job—that she could only do so much and not everything. Mothers are supposed to take care of their children and not the other way around.

She also saw that she never had had a real relationship with her mother, and she would never be able to have one. Now it would always be about bodily functions. They would never be connected on an emotional level. Painful as it was, she had to accept that this was the sum total of her relationship with her mother. She would have to look to other people to find healthy relationships, to have her needs met, to give and receive unconditional love. She had finally realized she couldn't get water from an empty well.

Nancy came from a very dysfunctional family and had been raised to take care of both her mother and father. As a child, love was conditional, and she had been emotionally abused. As she realized this she became angry about what she knew she would never receive from her mother. Nancy's anger became a healthy motivator to have her own needs met.

Years earlier, a counselor had asked, "Nancy, how do you feel?" She couldn't answer because she didn't know. Since then she has spent years looking into that question to discover how she actually feels, not how she should feel or thinks she should feel.

These days, Nancy makes a concerted effort not to take care of other people at the expense of her own needs. She has many friends and is always there for them. She is a loving and caring person, not out of guilt, not because she thinks she should be, but because this is who she is.

Now that she is not taking care of her mother, which had been almost a full-time job, she is beginning to focus on her own

needs. In fact, the first thing she did was to give up her private
practice as a therapist so she did not have to take care of others.

Nancy's new purpose is to follow her heart, to be herself
and to be all that she can be. She's finally ready to stop being
what she thinks other people want her to be.

Perfection

For it is only in the reality of our imperfection that
we can find the peace and serenity we crave.

—ERNEST KURTZ AND KATHERINE KETCHAM

A thirteenth-century Jewish mystic was approached by a disciple who wished to learn the art of meditation.

"Are you in a condition of perfect equilibrium?" asked the master.

"I think so," answered the disciple, who prayed regularly and practiced good deeds.

"When someone insults you, do you still feel injured? When you receive praise, does your heart expand with pleasure?"

The would-be disciple thought for a moment and replied somewhat sheepishly, "Yes, I suppose I do feel hurt when insulted and proud when praised."

"Well, then, go out and practice detachment from worldly pain and pleasure for a few more years. Then come back and I will teach you how to meditate."

Detachment from worldly pain and pleasure is a wonderful goal, but for us imperfect human beings, we must accept progress, not perfection—or we will carry the heaviness of disappointment, dissatisfaction and frustration in our hearts. We must accept ourselves just as we are. Remember our Heart-Lightening Process? First we *stop*, to bring ourselves into the present moment. Then we bring our full *awareness* to whatever is going on in the present moment. And then we *accept* whatever is going on in the present moment. This means everything, including ourselves. All our imperfections, our flaws, our quirks and our goodness and greatness.

This poem by the Sufi poet Rumi speaks eloquently about awareness and acceptance.

The Guest House

This being human is a guest house.
Every morning a new arrival.
A joy, a depression, a meanness,
some momentary awareness comes
as an unexpected visitor.
Welcome and entertain them all!
Even if they are a crowd of sorrows,
who violently sweep your house
empty of its furniture,
still, treat each guest honorably.
He may be clearing you out
for some new delight.

The dark thought, the shame, the malice,
meet them at the door laughing and invite them in.
Be grateful for whatever comes,
because each has been sent
as a guide from beyond.

If we deny any part of ourselves, if we close the door on the unwanted visitors, they stay to haunt us and shame us. By letting them into the lighted room of our hearts and embracing them all, without shame or judgment, we become free to live with light hearts. Ernest Kurtz and Katherine Ketcham write, "For to be human is to be incomplete. That it is human to be incomplete yet yearn for completion; it is to be uncertain, yet long for certainty; to be imperfect yet long for perfection; to be broken, yet crave wholeness." So how do we accept ourselves as we are when we continue to wish that we were different? Kurtz and Ketcham go on to say that this is perfectly human.

It was not until my late thirties, when I finally stopped drinking, that I began to know myself in even the smallest way. I discovered that there was the person I thought I was, the person I showed to others, and the real me—a stranger until then. A friend asked me to name five things that I disliked most about my now ex-husband. I listed them off in rapid succession. Easy! I could have listed ten more. Then she asked if I had any of those characteristics.

"Absolutely not," I answered with great assurance.

"Are you sure?" she pushed.

"Yes!" I exclaimed.

"Not one?" she pushed harder.

"Well," I paused long enough to reconsider. "Maybe a little of this and a bit of that." I can't even remember what those characteristics were now, but my ignorance and denial still amaze me. I had every one in varying degrees. It was as if a mirror had been held up so I could see my imperfections.

Later, I went on to do a searching and fearless moral inventory of the exact nature of my wrongs, which is the fourth of the twelve steps of self-help programs that follow the model of Alcoholics Anonymous. I began slowly uncovering the layers of ignorance and denial. At first I was appalled when I discovered I was self-centered and unforgiving. I could hold on to resentments and spend a long time in self-pity. Religion speaks of the seven deadly sins of anger, sloth, envy, pride, lust, greed and gluttony. At first, I felt embarrassed and ashamed to discover that, to some degree, I had committed all of them.

All spiritual practices advise us to look within ourselves. Author Thomas Keating tells us that the inward journey to our true self is the way to divine love. In the Twelve Steps and Twelve Traditions of Alcoholics Anonymous, step ten states: "It is a spiritual axiom that every time we are disturbed, no matter what the cause, there is something wrong with us." For many years I rebelled against this idea. What if someone insults me, or is mean to me? How is that my fault? It isn't, but how I feel about it is, and I learned that I can do something about how I react to it.

Author Thich Nhat Hanh explains that in the depths of our consciousness we have both the seeds of compassion and the seeds

of violence. He writes that we also have the seeds of understanding, forgiveness, mindfulness, fear and hatred.

By bringing our conscious awareness to what we are feeling in
each moment, we will discover that we do feel everything to some
degree or another. Only then can we choose how we want to act or
think, making the choice for what is in our best interests. Most of
us have probably never thought of torturing another human being,
but many of us, if we told the truth, have had thoughts such as,
You make me so mad I could hit you. While we may never mean to
act on them, such thoughts are there.

Self-Pity

*Self-pity is easily the most destructive
of the non-pharmaceutical narcotics: It is addictive,
gives momentary pleasure, and separates
the victim from reality.*

—JOHN GARDNER

"Poor me!" "No one likes me." "We never go anywhere." We
allow ourselves to sink deeper and deeper into the quagmire of
depression, looking for someone else to pull us out and make us
feel better. Self-pity and martyrdom go hand in hand. "Look how
hard I work!" "Look at all I've done for you!" And so on.

We're really saying: "Notice me." "Fix me." "Make me feel
better!" "If I don't show you or tell you how bad I feel, you'll never
feel sorry for me." Bill Wilson calls self-pity a bar to spiritual

progress since it can cut off effective communication with our fellows because of its inordinate demands for attention and sympathy. When we are in the power of self-pity we are totally self-centered. We are escaping from any responsibility as to why we feel the way we do. We blame life or other people.

When we can stop long enough to see this, to accept that we are creating our own unpleasant feelings, then we can take positive action steps. We can nurture ourselves. We can do a variety of things to lift our own spirits, take back our power and be in charge of our lives. This is how we grow and get better. Consider Butch's story.

If anyone could be filled with self-pity, Butch would be the one.

Over his lifetime, Butch has had three careers. First he was a chef at a nice restaurant, but he did a lot of drinking there, so he decided that he needed a change of environment. He began a new career as a plumber in a family business, but his alcoholic drinking continued. When he finally found sobriety, he knew he wanted to work with other recovering addicts, so he studied to become a licensed mental health counselor.

Butch loved his job, but found it increasingly difficult to process the paperwork necessary for it. He had notes all over the place to help him do ordinary tasks—if only he could have remembered to read them. Soon, Butch was forced to retire from the work that he loved because he was diagnosed with early-onset Alzheimer's disease.

This type of the disease is genetic and was first recognized when his family began noticing changes in their mother when she was around forty years old. She began going in and out of mental institutions, receiving shock treatments for what was diagnosed as depression. It was discovered later that she actually had early-onset Alzheimer's.

What is now known about the genetic, early-onset form of the disease is that it occurs in only fifteen percent of cases in which Alzheimer's disease exists, but when one parent does pass it down, as many as half of the children in the family can inherit it. As the disease progresses, the brain's nerve cells degenerate, and the brain itself actually shrinks in size, resulting in intellectual and personal decline and leading eventually to death. After Butch's mother died of the disease at age fifty-eight, the entire family was tested for predisposition to the disease. At least three, and possibly four of the children were found to have the gene.

In addition to early-onset Alzheimer's, there was quite a bit of alcoholism in Butch's family. Therefore, it was perfectly natural for Butch to become involved with drugs and alcohol at a very young age. Nobody at home could watch him because his mother's illness was so demanding, so he had free rein while he was in junior high and high school. In fact, Butch had begun drinking regularly by his freshman year in high school.

When Butch finally achieved sobriety, he began to notice he was having memory problems. He was forty years old. At first Butch's memory began to diminish just slightly, but in a short period of time he had a fifty percent memory loss. Since his diagnosis, half of his brain cells have deteriorated. Two of his sisters also came down with the disease. One died in her late fifties and the other in her mid-fifties.

It has been scary for Butch, but because of his strong belief in God and the tools he learned in recovery, he doesn't give up. He believes that God only wants the best for him.

How does anyone get through such a diagnosis, knowing that he is going to deteriorate mentally and die at a young age? With a new purpose born of necessity and love of each other, Butch, along with other members of his family, speak at symposiums and workshops. They try to educate the public about the disease, support those who have it and create support groups for other families. His family members are a wonderfully warm and loving support for each other.

Butch says that if it weren't for his sobriety and recovery program, he would still be out there drinking, and he certainly wouldn't be able to handle his life as it is today. Butch never feels alone or overwhelmed. He turns himself and his diseases over to God and tries his best to live one day at a time—and sometimes, one minute at a time.

Worry

If you worry, why pray and if you pray, why worry?

—Anonymous

Worry is one of the greatest barriers to peace of mind, joy and purpose. Worry blocks us from God. Worry and fear walk hand in hand. When we fear the outcome of a situation, our minds spin round and round, trying to find a solution. Worry creates stress, which blocks the healthy functioning of our minds. Stress can ultimately make us sick—mentally, physically and spiritually. Worry serves no purpose at all.

It is important to know that our bodies do not know the difference between something real or imagined. Therefore, our bodies respond to what is in our minds. For example, if we think that a tiger is going to walk through the door, our bodies go into stress mode. And if a tiger is really coming through the door, our bodies go into the same stress mode.

During stress, the release of chemicals is a survival mechanism that happens automatically in response to an emergency and prepares us for fight or flight. The chemicals released during stress affect our bodies in many ways: Adrenaline and noradrenaline are released into the bloodstream; the heart rate rises; metabolism increases, muscles become tense; breathing becomes rapid; and anxiety, hostility and anger increase.

This stress reaction can be triggered by a loud noise, by perceived or real danger, or by fear (false evidence appearing real) or a fearful thought. This reaction is especially important to understand because it influences our ability to solve problems. When we are in this state, our brain decreases the production of the faster beta waves and enhances the slower alpha, theta and delta waves. In effect, *our minds close down!*

Mindfulness, which we have learned about in the previous chapter, produces exactly the opposite results: Heart rate, metabolism, oxygen consumption and respiration decrease; blood pressure and muscle tension are lowered.

Simply bringing our awareness to our breathing can help us stop worrying, increase our clarity and help our minds to function. A simple solution to worry is to develop faith, which is discussed in the next chapter.

Artist Howard Chandler Christy wrote, "Every morning I spend fifteen minutes filling my mind full of God; and so there's no room left for worry thoughts."

The Heart-Lightening Process
Step 4:

CREATE AN INTENTION

*At each moment you choose the
intentions that will shape your experiences
and those upon which you will focus your
intention. These choices affect your evolutionary
process. This is so for each person.
If you choose unconsciously, you evolve
unconsciously. If you choose consciously,
you evolve consciously.*

—GARY ZUKAV

There are many steps we can take to let go of negative states, and they all begin with intention. Once we have the intention to change, the next step often flows without resistance. Sometimes we do know what to do, but we might not be willing to do it. We might need to make a change that is uncomfortable, such as leaving a job or giving up sweets. If this is the case, praying for the willingness to be willing really works! And if you are still unwilling, pray for the willingness to be willing to be willing. Take this to whatever degree works for you.

Willingness precedes action. Intention is thought. Thought is energy. Energy is action.

Affirmations

Affirmations are very helpful techniques that fortify our intentions and create change. Affirmations are simply positive statements we say to ourselves. As we are learning to observe our thoughts through the practice of mindfulness, we easily notice when it is time to change a thought. By changing our thinking we can change our attitudes. By changing our attitudes we can change our energy. And by changing our energy we can change our actions and thus change our lives. For example, if you become aware that you are thinking, *I'll never pass that exam*, which is a negative, energy-depleting thought, think instead, *I'm smart enough to pass my exam*! That is an energy-boosting thought.

It has been scientifically proven that the words we use can even make us healthy or sick. Brain wave tests prove that when we use positive words, our "feel good" neurotransmitters flow. Positive self-talk releases endorphins and serotonin in our brain, which then flow throughout our bodies, making us feel good. These neurotransmitters stop flowing when we use negative words.

To be successful, I have found that affirmations must have each of the following characteristics:

- They must be *positive*.
- They must be said and felt with *passion* and *power*.
- They must be framed in the *present moment*.
- They must be *possible*.
- They must be *personal*.

Repetition is also important. Write your affirmation ten times a day for twenty-one consecutive days. Many experiments have proven that change occurs within twenty-one days when we repeat something for twenty-one days. The following are some examples of affirmations that have been very successful for many people:

- God is guiding me to the perfect job for me.
- I am becoming willing to let go of my resentments.
- Healing energy is pouring through all the cells of my body.
- God gives me all the strength I need to handle my grief.

I have written much more about affirmations in the book *Change Almost Anything in 21 Days*,[6] if you would like to learn more about them. The following stories illustrate how two individuals used affirmations to powerful effect.

~

Tim had a huge obsession for sweets. He gained so much weight that his life was in danger. After attempting three or four diets and only lasting a short time with each one, he experimented with the following affirmation: "God gives me all the strength I need to eat only what is best for me." He began writing down this affirmation ten times a day, and after only four days he was offered a delicious-looking pie for dessert at a friend's house. He couldn't believe it when "No, thank you," came out of his mouth—and he really meant it!

Tim saw the change in his clothes within a week. He continued his writing for twenty-one days. Now he gives himself a sweet treat once in a while, but eats healthy food most of the time. He carries a slip of paper with his affirmation in his pocket, and when he gets the urge to indulge, he takes it out and reads it. It works for him!

~

These rules for affirmations are not cast in stone. Sometimes we have to adjust them for our particular circumstances. Nancy used affirmations in a different way from Tim, which was right for her. She was willing to do everything and anything to heal from her breast cancer.

~

"A couple of months after I'd started chemotherapy," Nancy wrote, "I saw Bernie Siegel speak. I'd seen him a couple of times, read one of his books and listened to some tapes, so I'd heard most of what he said before. What kept running through

my head after the talk was that I should 'give my body a live message.'

"It was September, and I was feeling, with good reason, that I might very well not see another fall. I wasn't even convinced that I'd see the following spring. Somehow, I wanted to tie my life to the future, pull my mind-set forward. That's why I end every day's affirmation writing with 'I will survive!!!' as opposed to 'I am surviving.' I want to throw a hook into the future.

"What do we do in the fall to remind us that spring will return? We plant bulbs, which is what I did. I planted bulbs, feeling that it would be a miracle if I were alive to see them bloom. Somehow, knowing those bulbs were under the ground waiting for spring helped lift my heart during that long winter (during which, by the way, my oncologist told me that I had already beaten the odds he had given me at diagnosis). When those bulbs burst through the soil I couldn't believe that I was on this planet to witness the event, and my heart was as light as a feather.

"Now you and I know that planting bulbs was not all I did that September to lift my heart, but it was one of the things, and it has become a symbol of hope for the future for me, which is why I'm picking up some more bulbs today!"

LETTING GO AFFIRMATION

*I've never learned anything
while I was talking.*

—LARRY KING

It is said that prayer is speaking to God and meditation is listening to God. If we are constantly asking for things or for advice, we have no idea what God has to say to us. For this we need quiet. We can reach a quiet place inside when we meditate. In this space we might not necessarily actually hear words from God, but we can come to a place of inner knowing. We can check in with our hearts, and our intuition can give us answers.

We need to take time to stop speaking to God, so we can listen, but we also need to stop the chattering that goes on in our minds. Bringing our awareness to our breath is a wonderful way to stop thoughts and quiet our minds so that we can tune in to messages from our higher power. God is always there for us. We simply need to stop and listen.

*Today I am taking time,
no matter what is going on in my life,
to spend some quiet time
with God.*

Filling Our Hearts
with Light

All other spiritual teachings are
in vain if we cannot love. Even the most
exalted states and the most exceptional spiritual accomplishments
are unimportant if we cannot
be happy in the most basic and ordinary ways,
if, with our hearts, we cannot touch
one another and the life we
have been given.

—Jack Kornfield

*I am grateful that not only can
I express joy unbounded but also that
I am able to express my grief and sadness as well.
My tears of release and pain soon become
tears of joy. My tears of grief and sadness soon
become tears of gratitude and wholeness.
Thank you, God, for the ability to
express all of my Divine Self!*

—*Science of Mind* MAGAZINE, MARCH 1989

W e begin first by stopping, then becoming aware and then accepting. We accept whatever we are feeling in the present moment. And in that acceptance, the miracle happens. The tension, the pain, the unhappiness begin to disappear and are replaced by peace. And in that peaceful space, compassion, faith, forgiveness, joy and love are uncovered. They were there all along. We were just looking in the wrong places.

Compassion

*Until he extends the circle of his
compassion to all living things, man
will not himself find peace.*

—ALBERT SCHWEITZER

One day while at the beach, I watched a little boy as he tried to play with two other boys in the water. They ignored him. Perhaps they had experienced his bullying before. He became very upset and then angry, splashing them with water before he headed for the beach. I remember thinking what a mean boy he was and turned back to my book, ignoring him.

The next time I saw him, I watched as he tagged along with some other kids, trying to get into their game. Maybe they had been told not to play with strangers. Maybe they had been hurt by him another time. I saw the longing on his face and his friendly smile turn to expressions of frustration and anger as they ignored him, whatever their reasons. He was hurt and rejected and called them names. When they continued to ignore him, in an effort to hurt them back, he grabbed a handful of sand and flung it at them.

As this was all happening I saw such clear evidence of his eagerness to become friends. I saw his yearning for connection. I saw his true essence, and my heart warmed to him, and I felt an outpouring of love and compassion. I wanted to hug him and hold him and tell him everything was going to be all right. I understood everything that followed. I understood him. Not that I liked him for his actions, but my feelings had changed toward him and I never wanted to go back to the way I felt before.

Not only did I like myself so much better as a compassionate person, it made me feel warm and open and light, whereas my feelings of judgment and disapproval left me cold and hard and closed.

It's important to accept that our hearts will not always be filled with compassion, no matter how much we wish it to be that way.

Accepting ourselves just as we are, without judgment, is our intention, and in doing so it lightens our hearts and allows compassion to enter. Author Christina Feldman wrote, "A compassionate heart is not an idealized heart that never experiences anger, greed or self-centeredness, but is the receptive presence that listens to those voices and receives them—without permitting them to be the guiding force of our actions, speech and choices."

The Dalai Lama defines compassion as "a state of mind that is nonviolent, non-harming, and non-aggressive. It is a mental attitude that is based on the wish for others to be free of their suffering and it is associated with a sense of commitment, responsibility and respect towards others." He believes that genuine compassion is based on the rationale that "all human beings have an innate desire to be happy, and overcome suffering, just like myself. . . . On the basis of the recognition of this equality and commonality, you develop a sense of affinity and closeness with others."

I always cry when something touches me, even commercials. I think I feel the sadness of others even more deeply since my son, Bob, died. I cry when I watch the evening news and they report that a child has drowned or a soldier was killed. I know what the parents must be going through.

A friend sent me this wonderful story titled "The Hungry Boy."

~~~

One day, a poor boy who was selling goods from door to door to pay his way through school found he had only one thin dime left, and he was hungry. He decided he would ask for a meal at the next house. However, he lost his nerve when a lovely young woman opened the door. Instead of a meal he asked for a drink of water. She thought he looked hungry so brought him a large glass of milk.

He drank it slowly, and then asked, "How much do I owe you?"

"You don't owe me anything," she replied. "Mother has taught us never to accept pay for a kindness."

"Then I thank you from my heart," he said. As Howard Kelly left that house, he not only felt stronger physically, but his faith in God and man was renewed. He had been ready to give up and quit.

Many years later that same young woman became critically ill. The local doctors were baffled. They finally sent her to the big city, where they called in specialists to study her rare disease. Dr. Howard Kelly was called in for the consultation. When he heard the name of the town she came from, a strange light filled his eyes. Immediately he rose and went down the hall of the hospital to her room. Dressed in his doctor's gown he went in to see her. He recognized her at once. He went back to the consultation room determined to do his best to save her life. From that day on he gave special attention to her case. And after a long struggle, the battle was won.

Dr. Kelly requested the business office to pass the final bill to him for approval. He looked at it, wrote something on the edge and the bill was then sent to the woman's room. She was afraid to open it, for she was sure it would take the rest of her life to pay for it all. Finally she looked, and something caught her attention on the side of the bill. She read these words: "Paid in full with one glass of milk, Dr. Howard Kelly."

Tears of joy flooded her eyes as her happy heart prayed: "Thank you, God, that your love has spread abroad through human hearts and hands."

When our hearts are open and we are connected to our feelings, we can be open to the joy and pain of others. Then we can experience, know or sense what someone else is going through. When this occurs, we can feel an undeniable connection, as if there were a direct line of energy connecting us with another person or with other people.

Faith

*Faith is the bird that sings when
the dawn is still dark.*

—RABINDRANATH TAGORE

I was told many years ago that faith is the opposite of fear. Fear is something we have when we are afraid that something is going to happen to us. Faith is knowing that everything is okay—no matter what will happen to us—in this present moment. And this present moment leads us to the next present moment, leads us to the next present moment . . . and our time for believing that everything is okay gets longer and longer. Faith is knowing that there is a divine plan, a plan much larger than ourselves. We don't have to know what it is. We just have to trust that we fit into this larger plan.

When I first tried to achieve sobriety, it was suggested that I ask for help from a power greater than myself, from a God I didn't believe in. I could not, until that point, with all my own power, stop drinking on my own. I was finally desperate enough to try anything. I prayed, "God, if you're there you will understand, and if you're not, it doesn't matter, but please keep me away from one drink for this day." That wasn't exactly faith. I was hedging, just in case there was a God, but I had a willingness to try anything. People told me to believe that they believed. I could do this because they told me that they, too, couldn't stop drinking until they prayed to this higher power.

Jim, a friend who has since passed away, gave me a wonderful visual example of faith. He said it was like walking through deep mud wearing hip-high boots in a fog so thick you couldn't see an inch in front of you and knowing that you would be safe taking the next step.

How do we have faith in the midst of fear? How, when things are not going our way, can we rely on faith? We can do it by knowing that there is a power greater than ourselves and then by becoming willing to connect with that power. We can feel it when we just stop and breathe. We can feel the energy. We can't see it. We can't taste it. But we can feel it. It becomes an inner knowing, an inner power that helps us get through the darkest hours. Faith lightens our hearts and replaces our worries.

It can be a faith in ourselves, in knowing that we have everything we need to take the next step, to do the next right thing. Buddha taught that suffering can be a springboard to faith. When we are in the midst of deep suffering, we can cry out to God or an unknown power and feel a release from our pain.

We can develop faith by reading inspirational books written over thousands of years. We can read more stories like those in chapter six of this book, which depict people going through the most difficult of times and managing to get through them because of their faith. We can pray to God to help us grow in faith. We can contemplate nature, observing that we have the same four seasons every year, and the same night and day every twenty-four hours.

Author Carolyn Myss writes, "Faith rests not only in hopes for the future, but also in the belief that 'all is as it should be'—here and now."

Fear closes us down. It changes the chemicals in our body. It depletes our energy. Faith reverses the process. It gives us strength. Faith is a spiritual awakening.

Janet recalls how faith got her through a difficult time in her life.

"It began when I chose to take on the world as a newly divorced, single mom with three children, ages nine, seven and five. One night, when I had finally had enough of struggling to

force things to happen, and after listening to a Carolyn Myss tape describing the 'Dark Night of the Soul,' I decided I had nothing to lose. Carolyn explained that spiritual growth never came easily, and that once in a while the universe required a leap of faith: Letting go and letting God was the only path to the other side.

"That night, I spoke to whoever was up there and let go of the reins. I asked God to take over my life, assuring him that I would listen to my intuition and follow my heart.

"The next day, a friend whom I hadn't really been in touch with in over two years arrived at my house to pick up her daughter. As we sat and talked, she shared how she could not find an administrative assistant. I knew at that moment that my prayers had been answered. I had found a job to support and provide for us.

"The job worked out nicely, and I was promoted to manager of the program after one year. I had that job for the next two years until a major shake-up occurred in the organization. Suffice it to say that it was evident I could no longer work at this company and maintain my integrity. Once again, I handed my life over to God. I chose to resign my position knowing full well I had no other immediate options.

"But once again, I trusted the universe. 'God,' I said, 'here we go again. I can't do this on my own, but with your help I know we'll be all right.' I gave the company three-months notice so they had plenty of time to fill my position.

"During the three months it took to separate from my old job, I looked and looked for work, but nothing appeared. Nothing happened. I ordered myself a new computer so I could work out of my home if necessary. I was spending money I

didn't have. Yet somehow, I knew deep inside that the universe would provide, and we would be fine.

"One night while meditating, the word 'hospice' kept coming to me. Following the Spirit's lead, I made an appointment with the head of the local hospice organization. We chatted, but no, they didn't have any jobs available, and I wasn't even sure why I was there. Nothing seemed to be falling into place. Christmas was coming, and I was going to be jobless.

"The unique story here is that deep inside, I was not worried. The universe had always held me in its arms, and this was no different. Have faith, it will come. Just follow the signs and trust the universe. *These were my mantras. And then it happened. The last day of my job, I sat at my desk and opened the local newspaper. It was the first thing I saw, at the bottom of the page: 'Hospice, Administrative Assistant.' It was mine. I knew it, and all I could feel was gratitude to the universe. I loved that job for the following two years, until the next step of my journey appeared.*

"The lesson here is that faith in the universe is the prerequisite for all things. Faith that the universe will provide exactly what you need when you live 'as light as a feather.' No worry to hold one down. No fear to darken the soul. When the heart speaks, life takes on new meaning, and provides you with exactly what you need."

Forgiveness—The Antidote for Guilt, Shame, Anger and Resentments

What could you want that forgiveness cannot give?

Do you want peace? Forgiveness offers it.

Do you want happiness, a quiet mind, a certainty of purpose, a
sense of worth and beauty that
transcends the world?

Do you want care and safety and the warmth of sure protection
always?

Do you want a quietness that can't be disturbed, a gentleness that
never can be hurt, a deep
abiding comfort, and a rest so perfect it can never be upset?

All this forgiveness offers you.

—A Course in Miracles

It is normal to feel anger when someone has done us harm or when it appears that someone has done us harm. Anaïs Nin writes, "We don't see things as they are, we see them as we are." It is common to feel anger when we hear about rape and murder and torture. Anger is a natural emotion that serves us well sometimes for survival. As said before, anger is usually a cover-up for fear. We are afraid of losing something we already have, or afraid that we are not going to get something we want.

How many of us can really forgive the likes of Hitler, Saddam Hussein and Osama bin Laden, even though we know that holding on to anger and resentment damages us physically, mentally and spiritually? Ancient wisdom as well as all spiritual laws tell us forgiveness must be our goal, our intention. If we are to come to a place of peace in our hearts, we must come from a place of willingness. To me this means that we can feel our anger, acknowledge our anger and then let it go. For addicts especially, holding on to anger will ultimately lead to picking up a drink, drug or food, among other things.

In the Sermon on the Mount, Jesus tells us we must pray to forgive ourselves as we forgive those who trespass against us. "As we forgive those . . ." is the key here. We can't be forgiven unless we forgive others. We hear this from the pulpit. We read about it in the writings of mystics, saints and sages. But how can we forgive when we know that Hitler killed eleven million human beings, when Saddam Hussein used gas to kill thousands of his own people? When bin Laden was the force behind the devastating tragedy of September 11, 2001?

Perhaps on our own we can never completely forgive. But we can be willing. We can learn about the value of forgiveness and pray for willingness, or we will never lighten our hearts. Confucius tells us that "to be wronged is nothing unless you continue to remember it."

A friend of mine was once deeply hurt by a sister who had betrayed her. My friend said she would never, never forgive her sister for what she had done to her. She had such anger and hate that when she told the story, her face became red and her breathing rapid. I worried for her health. When I suggested that she try to forgive her sister, she turned her anger on me. "Never!" she exclaimed and walked out of the room. She had no idea how much harm she was doing to herself.

Anne had to learn her lessons about the power of forgiveness over and over again.

~

For many years Anne carried the weight of anger, resentment and self-justification in her heart. In Anne's early twenties, her best friend had decided not to come to her wedding because of a misunderstanding. After arguing with her about it, Anne made a decision not to talk to her ever again. This is the way she used to deal with anger and resentments.

Years later, Anne fought for joint custody of her children during a very painful divorce—and lost. One day she went to visit her children. She sat in her car, alone and in a rage, in the driveway of what was once her home, but now belonged to her ex-husband. His car was in the driveway, too, which meant that he was home. Anne was so angry and the situation was so painful that she couldn't bring herself to go into the house while he was home. She drove out of the neighborhood and called her children from a phone booth to let them know that she couldn't see them that day. That was one of the most painful days of her life.

Anne knew this anger was not good for her and certainly not good for any relationship she might have with her children. She asked friends for advice and was told, "What? Forgive him? After what he did to you?"

Everyone suffered by her hanging on to this resentment. It still took her a few years to make any attempt to let her rage go. She first had to pray for the willingness, knowing that she could not reach that step without help from a power greater than herself.

Ernest Kurtz and Katherine Ketcham, in their book *The Spirituality of Imperfection,* point out that the word for-*give*-ness connotes a gift. We are giving ourselves a gift when we become willing to forgive. The authors go on to say that to forgive does not mean to forget, quoting the words of psychiatrist Thomas Szasz: "The stupid neither forgive nor forget; the wise forgive, but they do not forget."

A former inmate of a Nazi concentration camp was visiting a friend who had shared the ordeal with him.

"Have you forgiven the Nazis?" he asked his friend.

"Yes."

"Well I haven't. I'm still consumed with hatred for them."

"In that case," said his friend gently, "they still have you in prison."

There are some situations that cannot be helped, no matter how willing we are to make amends. The following story illuminates that truth.

~

A young man in a certain village maliciously spread gossip about another in the village. Soon after the incident, the man regretted what he had said and went to his rabbi for advice on how to make right the wrong that he had committed. The rabbi sent him on a task. He told the man to fill a pillowcase with feathers and walk around to each door of every home in the village and place a feather on the steps in front of the door.

The man did not understand how this would make him feel better, but he listened and obliged the rabbi. After he had finished he came back to the rabbi.

"I did as you asked, but I do not feel any better, nor do I understand the purpose of this task," stated the man. The rabbi told him he was not yet done with the task. Then he told the man to go back to each home and gather up the feathers and place them back in the bag.

The man did as the rabbi said, but soon became very frustrated: As he approached each home, he found the feather was no longer there. The wind had blown it away.

He came back with an empty bag and told the rabbi the feathers were nowhere to be found.

"Good," said the rabbi. "Now you have learned the lesson. You see, words are like those feathers. When you misuse words and repeat gossip, it spreads and flies through the community like those feathers. The words can never be taken back, just as the feathers cannot be collected." With that, the man realized he could not undo what he had done. He could only resolve to never again spread rumors or gossip.

I remember attending a workshop many years ago where I was overcome with a feeling of shame. The presenter suggested that we let our hearts stretch a little bigger to let in more love. I had this sudden feeling of shame, knowing that my heart was still full of anger against my father. At the time, I was leading workshops of my own, and I felt like a fake. How could I teach meditation, compassion and forgiveness when I had not forgiven my father? I knew forgiveness was the answer, but I had not been able to accomplish it, no matter how hard I prayed.

I rarely saw my father after that scene when I ripped up the bank card in the hospital. I saw him, of course, at my mother's funeral, and I helped move him to an assisted-living apartment later. Years went by, and we had very little contact. Somehow, I heard he was sick. While driving to the hospital to visit him before putting him in a nursing home, I listened to a tape by Elizabeth Kübler Ross on forgiveness. One of the stories she told was called "Unfinished Business."

You remember when I insisted we go to the beach and you said, "No. It's going to rain"?

And I absolutely insisted and you said, "It's going to be a horrible day," and didn't want to go? But I insisted and we went and it was a horrible day and it rained all day and I thought you were really going to give me hell for it.

But you didn't.

Remember when I tried to make you jealous and I went out with another boy? I thought this time you're really going to drop me.

But you didn't.

Remember when I demanded that we go to this dance and you didn't want to come but I demanded it? I also forgot to tell you that it was formal? And you came in jeans? I thought "You're gonna kill me!"

But you didn't.

I wanted to tell you all these things when you came home from Vietnam.

But you didn't.

Something shifted inside of me when I heard that tape, and I began to cry. I knew I was changed by it. Today I know that I had a spiritual awakening as a result. I went into my father's hospital room and we talked. I can't remember what we spoke about, but afterward I do remember he said, "I was nervous about you coming here. I didn't know how it was going to go. We haven't seen each other for so long. It's your fault, you know."

Ordinarily I would have argued with him, finding a way, at least in my mind, to blame him. Instead, I looked at him and answered, in words that did not feel as if they were coming from me, "I know."

When I left his room, tears were streaming down my face. A woman asked me if I was all right.

"Yes," I answered quietly. "I just forgave my father."

Later, in the elevator, someone else asked if I was all right. "I just forgave my father," I told her.

Still, we were never close after that. He remained a difficult, argumentative person. Later, I was able to do what had to be done to move him to a comfortable nursing home and visit him regularly until he died. I could be pleasant and not respond to his stubbornness. Mother Teresa wrote, "People are often unreasonable, illogical and self-centered. Forgive them anyway." I no longer carried the years of anger and fear and resentments. My heart was much lighter. Healing had finally taken place.

Let us not forget about self-forgiveness, about becoming willing to let go of all the things for which we beat ourselves up, all the shame and guilt we carry as a heavy weight within our hearts. A few years after my son, Bob, died, I was ready to do some deep soul-searching around the areas of my life that might have contributed to his death.

A very wise therapist had told me that no matter the cause of the death, when a child takes his own life, it is the most natural thing in the world for a mother to blame herself. We could have done this or not done that, or we could have done this or that better. An extreme example she gave me was of a parent who blamed herself for not going to one of her son's Cub Scout meetings.

I went off by myself in a camper and spent a few days in solitude. I let myself remember everything that I ever did or didn't do for and to my son. I did a thorough, soul-searching examination of my life, knowing that some of my actions certainly did contribute to his unhappiness. I could not deny this, no matter how many times people said to me that Bob made his own choice to leave this earth. My alcoholism and divorce were painful for any child to live through. I had to own it, accept it and forgive myself. I prayed and I meditated, asking for help to be honest and thorough.

Years later, I found an old note I had written to myself while trying to deal with the guilt I felt around the death of my son. At that time I still carried a great deal of anger toward my ex-husband. The note simply said, "Done the best I could. If I say this, then so has he."

As I look at this many years later I have a feeling of peace, a light heart. Haven't we all done our best? Even if we're not satisfied with some of our actions, weren't they the best we could do at the time? We could say, "I should have done this or that, or I could have done better." But these statements come from hindsight. Whatever we did, we did. This is simply acceptance.

Accept the past as it is, a memory of an action, thought, situation or mood. When we bring the past into the present moment, we interrupt our peace. We add heaviness to our hearts.

We can never recreate the actual event because when we bring the past into the present moment, we look at it filtered through the eyes of judgment, rationalizations and self-justification, and with the new knowledge we have gained since that time. Or we see the past event exaggerated or diminished because of our feeling attached to the situation.

In order to be free we need to ask for forgiveness as well as give it. "Forgive us our trespasses as we forgive those who trespass against us," we pray in the Lord's Prayer. Catholics use confession as a way of clearing their hearts. Jews have Yom Kippur—the Day of Atonement—once a year to deeply examine their lives and ask God for forgiveness.

Asking God for forgiveness is not enough to truly clear our hearts. We have to go to the individual person or persons we have harmed whenever possible, so we will not have barriers or walls between ourselves and others.

Asking forgiveness in a letter is most helpful if someone you have hurt has died, and you are still carrying feelings of guilt and shame. Write a sincere letter as if you are truly writing to this person. The key here is that you would be willing to make amends if it were possible.

Living light as a feather is about being free enough to walk down any street and not fear that we might meet someone to whom we owe money, or who we have harmed in any way.

Here is a wonderful story on forgiveness and healing.

~

Build Bridges Not Fences

Once upon a time two brothers who lived on adjoining farms fell into conflict. It was the first serious rift in forty years of farming side by side, sharing machinery, and trading labor and goods as needed without a hitch. Then the long collaboration fell apart. It began with a small misunderstanding, it grew into a major difference, and finally it exploded into an exchange of bitter words followed by weeks of silence.

One morning there was a knock on John's door. He opened it to find a man with a carpenter's toolbox.

"I'm looking for a few days work," he said. "Perhaps you would have a few small jobs here and there I could help with? Could I help you?"

"Yes," said the older brother. "I do have a job for you. Look across the creek at that farm. That's my neighbor—in fact, it's my younger brother. Last week there was a meadow between us and he took his bulldozer to the river levee and now there is a creek between us. Well, he may have done this to spite me, but I'll go him one better. See that pile of lumber by the barn? I want you to build me a fence—an eight-foot fence—so I won't need to see his place or his face anymore."

The carpenter said, "I think I understand the situation. Show me the nails and the post-hole digger and I'll be able to do a job that pleases you."

The older brother had to go to town, so he helped the carpenter get the materials ready and then he was off for the day. The carpenter worked hard all that day, measuring, sawing, nailing. About sunset when the farmer returned, the carpenter had just finished his job. The farmer's eyes opened wide, his jaw dropped. There was no fence there at all. It was a bridge—a bridge stretching from one side of the creek to the other! A fine piece of work, handrails and all—and the neighbor, his younger brother, was coming across, his hand outstretched.

"You are quite a fellow to build this bridge after all I've said and done."

The two brothers stood at each end of the bridge, and then they met in the middle, taking each other's hand. They turned to see the carpenter hoist his toolbox on his shoulder.

"No, wait! Stay a few days. I've a lot of other projects for you," said the older brother.

"I'd love to stay on," the carpenter said "but I have many more bridges to build."

—⌒⌒

Generosity

If you knew what I know about the power of giving, you would not let a single meal pass without sharing it in some way.

—BUDDHA

The Buddha teaches that there are three kinds of giving. The first one is tentative giving: "I don't really need this any more. Should I keep it or give it away?" We learn, when we do give it away, that there is some joy in our hearts from this act. The next is friendly giving: We share something because we have enjoyed it, and we want to pass it on for others' enjoyment. This can be our time or our things and this gives us even more joy. The third level is kingly or queenly giving: This is the giving of ourselves, our time, our energy and also of things that mean a great deal to us. This gives us great joy.

There's a wonderful story by an unknown author about a wise woman and a precious stone.

A wise woman who was traveling in the mountains found a precious stone in a stream. The next day she met another traveler who was hungry, and the wise woman opened her bag to share her food.

The hungry traveler saw the precious stone and asked the woman to give it to him. She did so without hesitation. The traveler left rejoicing in his good fortune. He knew the stone was worth enough to give him security for a lifetime. But, a few days later, he came back to return the stone to the woman.

"I've been thinking," he said. "I know how valuable this stone is, but I give it back in the hope that you can give me something even more precious. Please give me what you have within you that enabled you to give me this stone."

Another story I heard years ago at a retreat clearly illustrates the value of generosity.

A man is graced with a vision of the afterlife. He is first shown a great hall with a long banquet table filled with ambrosial delights. Each diner is equipped with a three-foot-long spoon, but no matter how much they contort their arms, thrusting their elbows into their neighbors' faces, their utensils are too long to maneuver even a single morsel into their gaping mouths. They sit together, opposite and side by side, in mutual misery. "This," says the man's otherworldly guide, "is hell."

The visitor is then taken to another place and sees an identical banquet table set with the same sumptuous food and the

*same impossible silverware. Only here the people are well fed,
utterly joyous, glowing with health and well-being. "This," pro-
nounces the host, "is Heaven."*

The man is baffled. "What's the difference?"

*"In Heaven," says the guide, pointing delightedly as a per-
son lifts his long-handled spoon across the table to the parted
lips of a neighbor, "they feed each other."*

In Judaism, there are deeds called loving-kindnesses. I was so
touched by one I heard about—that farmers leave unharvested
produce in the corners of the field for the poor and for strangers.
Others include feeding the hungry, clothing the naked, comforting mourners and showing deference to the aged.

Generosity does not only mean giving something material
away. Generosity of spirit is a wonderful gift we can develop.
Sometimes it's not what you have but what's inside you that others
need. Generosity with our time is just as important as material
generosity and just as difficult at times. Listening deeply, the giving of advice when asked for, compassion, understanding, support,
and encouragement can change another person's life.

What happened to Rabbi Mazo is a wonderful example of
generosity of the spirit and compassion and faith.

*Rabbi Gary Mazo met Rabbi Fred Neulander and his
wife, Carol, in 1983 when he and his wife-to-be, Debbi, were*

students at Brandeis University. Debbi, who was searching for
a spiritual home, happened upon Congregation M'kor Shalom,
which means "Source of Peace."

Subsequently, Rabbi Neulander became Rabbi Mazo's
mentor and role model when he was hired to work for him after
his ordination in 1990. He was quickly given more and more
responsibility as the senior rabbi began pulling back from the
day-to-day responsibilities of the temple. By 1994 Rabbi Mazo
had made the decision to leave M'kor Shalom and move toward
his own dreams and goals. However, on Tuesday, November 1,
1994, Rabbi Mazo's life and the life of his congregation
changed forever. That night, Carol Neulander was found bru-
tally murdered in her home.

Her family, the congregation and the entire community
went into shock. The communal grief was unlike anything the
rabbi had ever experienced in his short career in the rabbinate.
The next day, a thousand mourners came to the synagogue for
a memorial service. The following day, two thousand attended
the funeral. Everyone was existing in a surreal world, not truly
believing what they were going through. As the traditional
seven day period of mourning, known as shiva, *got underway,*
grief mingled with fear and anger. Almost immediately, charges
of personal misconduct and sexual impropriety formed a cloud
over the grieving widower.

"Allegations of his involvement in the murder itself soon
rocked the very core of our souls. I found myself in the middle
of what seemed a terrible made-for-TV movie. But this was
real," said Rabbi Mazo.

"Within months, while no formal charges were filed in
connection with the murder, the rabbi resigned in disgrace
amidst continued allegations of misconduct. As the associate

rabbi at Congregation M'kor Shalom, I suddenly found myself responsible for the spiritual well-being of a thousand bewildered families. Under normal circumstances, I would probably not have assumed the role of primary spiritual leader to a congregation of that size for another twenty years. I was facing what would certainly be the greatest challenge of my career. Before it was over, we would all struggle with our faith, with God and with Judaism.

"The Bible tells us that when Moses was fleeing the house of Pharaoh he happened upon a certain bush in the desert. As he looked closer, Moses saw the bush was burning yet the flames did not consume it. Moses stopped, looked into the flames and was able to find there the presence of God. That was our task: to keep hold of our faith amidst the flames which could very well have consumed us."[1]

Rabbi Mazo wrestled with how to meet the needs of a bruised community, often feeling afraid and inadequate. Part of his goal was to "help the congregation begin to see the opportunity in the midst of the flames of crisis."

In his book, And the Flame Did Not Consume Us, *he chronicles the "spiritual challenge, emotional upheaval and personal journey the congregation and I experienced through this turbulent time. . . . My goal was twofold: to offer tribute to the power of the human spirit, which was displayed by so many throughout this ordeal; and to demonstrate the power of Judaism to provide light and guidance in the aftermath of tragedy. It is my hope that other faith communities will find strength and renewal from our journey through the valley of darkness."*

Rabbi Neulander was eventually arrested for the murder of his wife. When people saw the rabbi on TV in prison garb,

*many cried. He had been their trusted and revered spiritual
leader. It was a tormenting and incomprehensible vision.*

*Sometimes Rabbi Mazo felt paralyzed with fear. He
couldn't share his own inner pain and struggle with his congregation, and he felt grossly inadequate to the task of shepherd-
ing his congregation through this communal nightmare. But,
as he explains, grieving is only "truly complete by learning and
understanding."*

*Rabbi Mazo is a powerful example of how we can go .
through an excruciatingly painful time and find a greater purpose in it. In his last sermon to his congregation, Rabbi Mazo
said that they had survived and thrived because they were a
family: "We looked into the dark shadows and found light."*

Gratitude

**If the only prayer you ever say in your entire
life is thank you, it will be enough.**

—MEISTER ECKHART

The Talmud says: "When Nebuchadnezzar, the mighty King
of Babylonia, wanted to sing praises to God, an angel came and
slapped him in the face." Asked the Kotzker, "Why did he deserve
to be slapped if his intention was to sing God's praises?" He
answered himself, "You want to sing praises while you are wearing
your crown? Let me hear how you praise me having been slapped
in the face."

When we are going through a painful time, or we are not getting what we want, gratitude is one of the hardest things to even consider. How can we possibly be grateful when the world isn't going our way? Or when we are angry or depressed or full of fear? Yet, gratitude is the one thing that can change our mood, our perception, even our outlook in almost an instant.

I use a wonderful exercise for gratitude that will work every time, if we have the willingness. When going through a difficult time, find three reasons for which to be grateful for something that tests you. While writing this book, I had an excellent example of this. I broke my toe, but I could easily find three things about that for which I was grateful. One, it happened to my left foot so I could still drive. Two, it was in the autumn, so I didn't have to worry about falling on snow or ice. And three, I was in the midst of writing this book, which meant I was sitting at my computer most of the day and I could rest my toe so it could heal.

I've taught this principle in my mediation classes and have enjoyed watching the tense faces of those who have tried it relax and fill with smiles. Mary, for example, was having a terrible time with a self-centered, controlling mother-in-law. Yet, she could see how she learned patience, tolerance and acceptance as she tried to deal with the woman in a healthy manner.

Gratitude removes our tensions, softens our heart and allows us to feel love and joy. Gratitude lists are wonderful to make on a daily basis. They are very comforting to read during the days when gratitude is difficult to find. Sarah Ban Breathnach writes in her book *Simple Abundance,* "You simply will not be the same person two months from now after consciously giving thanks each day for the abundance that exists in your life. And you will have set in motion an ancient spiritual law: The more you have and are grateful for, the more will be given you."

Kathi's story illustrates how gratitude can help us turn around a painful loss and find a new purpose.

⌒

In 1988, Kathi's husband, Mead, had an accident while on Block Island off Rhode Island and had to be transported back to the mainland. Mead became semi-paralyzed. Kathy remembers that they had plans to do something that weekend with some friends, and she was furious at him for being the cause of their changing plans. But she was also shocked that she could have so much anger when he was so sick, and it wasn't his fault.

Their social structure crumbled because of this accident, and Kathi went into a period of despair. She couldn't talk to her husband. Instead, she used alcohol obsessively to run away from the pain she was feeling. She had periodically used alcohol in the past when she was going through a hard time, and this time sought out counseling to get some help.

Her social worker directed her to a program of recovery, showing her that she was alcohol dependent. Kathi went through this difficult time alone. She had no friends and felt abandoned by God. She continued to go to church, convinced that if she were a better person, bad things wouldn't happen to her.

Kathi was still very angry—grieving over the loss of alcohol in her life and her husband's illness. It took him a long time to recover and during this process he didn't feel like doing anything. Her older daughter was off to college and it was very lonely.

Around the time of her husband's fiftieth birthday and her parents' fiftieth wedding anniversary, Kathi's younger, nineteen-year-old daughter, Kerry, started to feel very sick. The doctors determined she had mononucleosis, an autoimmune disease caused by the Epstein-Barr virus. Very quickly Kerry's condition worsened. They took blood tests and hospitalized her. Her systems were shutting down and the doctors said they might lose her. They tried everything. Finally, they had to intubate her to help her breathe, but it also prevented her from talking. After six or seven torturous days, Kerry died. It all happened so fast, within one week.

During the process, Kathi started praying for faith. She knew there was no bargaining with God. She knew there was nothing she could do to make it right, but she started going to daily mass as a way of meditating. She had been working hard on her spirituality for the prior three years and knew the concept of staying in the moment. So she would get on her knees repeatedly and turn her daughter over to God and the care of the doctors.

When Kerry died, Kathi remembers being aghast. "Oh my God. She died and I'm okay." Kathi was emotionally and physically exhausted and settled into a numbness that protected her. Her golf and support group friends were wonderfully supportive, but she remembers being very disappointed that no one from the church supported her through her grief.

She didn't have much energy to do a lot of things. Yet, even though she was still in a great deal of pain, a part of her was *serene. She knew she was being taken care of through it all. It always seemed that when she had a blue day, someone would call to cheer her up. What helped her tremendously was to connect with others who were in pain and try to help them. It contributed enormously to her recuperation.*

Kathi had a job teaching English as a second language to hospital employees. She would prepare for her classes, cry all the way to the hospital, and then when she arrived, she would enter a small chapel and say a few prayers. It acted like a switch being turned on for her to stop crying and start teaching. The people that she was teaching were so grateful that they helped her to feel buoyed up.

It is a slow healing process for Kathi. She gradually began putting new activities back into her life. It helped to read books on grief. She talked daily to two new friends who shared similar grief. One had recently lost a father, the other a brother. As anyone who has gone through it knows, recovery from grief is progressive but not necessarily continuous. Some days are good while others seem to put one back at the beginning of the loss.

Kathi has struggled with God during this painful time. Did God call Kerry home, she questioned? If God is really omnipotent, he could have chosen not to take her. And if he is omnipotent, why did he choose to call her?

During the healing process, Kathi has come to the realization that Kerry had been a wonderful gift for nineteen years. She feels that she must have been very special to have been such a gift.

Through it all, Kathi has become stronger and has learned to speak up for herself. When someone told her, as they inevitably did, that it was time to move on with her life, she would say she wasn't ready and continued to work with others.

She met a woman who had lost two daughters and they began a grief group that met once a month. Kathi continued to make herself available to others who had lost children. She knows how difficult it often is for other people to talk about death, especially when time has passed since the loss. There is a deep avoidance in our society around talking about death. But, Kathi is always there to listen. Her next-door neighbor lost a child and Kathi grieved with her. She has learned that when helping others, they are inadvertently helping her.

At first, friends came to her to see how they could help. But soon people stopped coming and many drifted out of her life. She's made new special relationships. Knowing that Kerry would want her to, she has tried to live life more fully.

In Kerry's honor, Kathi and her husband, Mead, donated a bench on the town green with Kerry's graduating class date engraved on it. They have begun a fund to send children with cancer to a special camp, and have had a cabin built at that camp in Kerry's name. They lent their support to her sorority's effort to set up a scholarship fund to help a young woman in Kerry's sorority.

Friends introduced Kathi to people who had lost children some years earlier. She saw that some of them were still fixated on the death. The successful ones who were able to get on with their lives were the ones who had a strong faith.

Kathi knows that spiritual practice requires discipline. When she was still so raw, she felt joy and pain more intensely. Now she is in a place of contentment, serenity and joy. She is much quieter and knows that everything is okay.

Joy

Angels fly because they take
themselves so lightly.

—Anonymous

Four years before my son, Bob, died, I wrote *Time for Joy*, a daily meditation book. After his death, I remember being very upset with myself for a time. *How could I have written such a book*, I asked myself. *We can't always have joy. There can be months when we don't experience joy. How could I have let people think that joy was as simple as I wrote?*

It took time, reading, soul-searching and speaking with many people to come back to know what I had always known, that joy lives inside of each and every one of us. Spiritual author Karen Casey put this so well when she wrote, "My life here today and all my tomorrows will give me as much joy as my heart can contain."

We need to allow ourselves to feel everything, to go through all the stages of our grief, to feel our pain, to express our anger and our disappointments in a healthy way. We empty so that we can refill. We express so that we have the room to allow joy and peace to enter our hearts. Charlotte Joko Beck writes, "Joy is who we are if we are not preoccupied with something else."

All spiritual teachers tell us that we are full of love and joy. Our lesson on this earth is to discover and remove the barriers that keep up from knowing and experiencing this. Joy can exist with pain and fear and grief, because joy is always with us, in our hearts and in our souls. We can be experiencing great suffering and still connect with joy at a very deep level, knowing that we are not alone, that God is with us and a part of us at all times.

So while we might not actually be able to feel joy at all times, we can come to know that joy lies deep within us, perhaps just a breath away. It might present itself for just a brief moment, to help ease our suffering. It might sneak into our consciousness when we see a rainbow, or have a pleasant memory of someone who has died, or receive a hug from a friend or feel a connection to our higher power. There can be joy in knowing that God is in charge, and with this knowledge we know we can get through anything. And that gives us lighter hearts.

Although it is not easy to see humor when we are in pain, for those of us who are lucky enough to be able to do this, humor can help us get through many difficult times. Allen Klein writes that "humor can help us cope with the unbearable so that you can stay on the bright side of things until the bright side actually comes along." Humor can help heal our immune systems, which suffer when we are under a great deal of stress. Laughter is a wonderful way to release pent-up emotions so that we can feel lighter.

Eckhart Tolle, in his book *The Power of Now,* wrote that pleasure is always derived from something outside of you, whereas joy arises from within. He says that the very thing that gives you pleasure today will give you pain tomorrow, or it will leave you, so its absence will give you pain. "As soon as you honor the present moment," he writes, "all unhappiness and struggle dissolve, and life begins to flow with joy and ease."

Ellen's story illustrates the healing power that laughter and embracing each moment provides. She has found that even with all the pain she experiences, she can still find joy.

~~~~

Ellen was a successful entrepreneur, the very heart of the organization she worked for. She was a team builder, and with her loving, tender spirit she knew how to keep people happy, and her company grew.

At forty-two years old, Ellen was in very good health. It came as a shock, then, when she discovered she had lung cancer, already in Stage 3B. She didn't have a primary tumor; instead, cancer cells were spread throughout her lungs and couldn't be removed by surgery. She needed to have chemotherapy.

To help get through this difficult time, Ellen did something extraordinary. She threw chemo parties, or hootenannies, as she called them, for all the patients who were going through chemotherapy. The hospital was very cooperative about this because her parties really boosted morale for both staff and patients. Ellen coordinated everything. She found a guitar player and a singer to join her, and they played and sang to everyone all the time they were going through their chemotherapy. There could be thirty people in the room at any given moment, all sharing a joyous time.

It took Ellen eighteen months to recover from her ordeal and she celebrated finishing her chemotherapy and finally feeling better by going skiing with her daughter.

But her difficulties were not over. For six months she had to go through very difficult radiation treatments. It left her with no energy, and she was not able to do anything for herself.

Fortunately, her mom and dad were able to come and help her through it.

In fact, she had what she calls "many little angels" to help her. The Temple Sisterhood coordinated her meals and they were wonderful to her, bringing her so much food she had to get a second refrigerator.

Ellen had always been the giver, the doer for others. Now she learned to receive, to accept from people. This went on for six months.

By August Ellen began doing quite well. Her energy came back and she was able to give a luncheon for her fiftieth birthday; sixty-five people came to celebrate with her.

Unable to return to work because of a damaged nerve, she received a permanent disability. After all she had been through, Ellen found herself asking, "Who am I?" Her ability to walk up and down stairs was limited and she always found herself to be on the wrong floor. Her husband, Larry's, love is unconditional and he said, "I will follow you anywhere." So she and Larry decided to sell their house and move to Florida.

Sadly, cancer recurred. It had metastasized to Ellen's liver. She tried everything she could to get through it, including Reiki, reflexology, visualizations and chemotherapy. She even threw her hootenanny parties again.

Her cancer recurred in the liver four times, and as if this weren't enough, in the midst of her treatment, her husband lost his job because his company was downsizing as a result of the events of September 11. Since Larry has such a passion for running diagnostics on computers, Ellen encouraged him to do what he loved and he came up with his own company called The Computer Guy.

Ellen does his advertising and marketing. After the first year Larry had enough work to keep him busy ten to twenty hours a week. Since he is semiretired, they are both really enjoying life. Ellen says that now life feels like a fairy tale, an adventure complete with wonderful new friends in Florida. A very special gift came when Ellen was invited to celebrate a b'not mitzvah with her daughter, which is a bas mitzvah that takes place for several females at the same time.

When her cancer recurred for a fourth time, Ellen was living in Florida. In order for her insurance to cover the costs, she had to fly back to Boston for her chemotherapy, traveling three weeks out of four for months. The free tickets she was able to solicit from some of the airlines helped considerably. When people heard of her travel predicament, they began donating frequent flyer miles to her. The local newspaper picked up the story and started a prayer list for her; more donations came in. After all her traveling, the cost was only $400 out of her pocket. People in Boston opened their homes to her when she came for treatment, so she also never had the expense of a car rental or a motel.

Ellen is full of so much gratitude. She has gone from a person who was the one in charge to being a person who is able to receive and accept and trust others. She has been given a new opportunity to love people in her life.

Ellen believes her change in attitude blossomed because of attending personal growth workshops to get through a painful divorce when she was thirty-five years old.

"I don't allow cancer to define me or rule me. I live a life-affirming existence. I've chosen a path to enjoy an enriched quality of life that includes meeting new people and making a difference in their lives. This means I include them so that

they, too, can make self-discoveries and develop greater personal awareness."

Where before she went in pain, Ellen now goes in joy.

~~~

Love

Someday, after we have mastered the winds,
the waves, the tides and gravity, we shall
harness for God the energies of love. Then,
for the second time in the history of the world,
man will have discovered fire.

—Teilhard de Chardin

I saw the words of Teilhard de Chardin on the blackboard of a class I was taking when I went to graduate school in my late forties, and I was deeply moved. Until that time, I had considered there to be three kinds of love; the first was the love one has, at the highest level, for God; at the next level was love for parents, children, and friends; the third kind was romantic love.

It took me a long time to discover the profoundness of what occurred when I read those words, but I know I understood the transformational power of love for the first time.

Now I know that the love de Chardin speaks of is a spiritual love—not the love of a specific someone or some thing, but a feeling that is not attached to anything, that just is. We can reach deep within us whenever we choose and find that power, once we have cleared the layers that have blocked us from feeling it.

Love, like joy, is as much a part of us as are our hearts and our brains. Love is an enormous energy. When we feel it, we are moved by it and can move others by it if they are receptive. Our job is to unlearn all the low-energy emotions that keep us down, blocking us from feeling the incredible power of love.

Mother Teresa said, "Joy is prayer; joy is strength; joy is love; joy is a net of love by which you can catch souls."

The Heart-Lightening Process
Step 5:

AWAKEN SPIRITUALLY

There is a God-shaped vacuum in the heart of every person, and it can never be filled by any created thing. It can only be filled by God.

—BLAISE PASCAL

How do we go from fear to love? How do we go from a sense of powerlessness to a feeling of power? How do we grow into the person we want to be when all our efforts in the past have failed? The first step is to connect with God, Allah, Universal Energy, Spirit, whatever we choose to call our higher power. This is the key that fits into the keyhole that opens the door to joy and purpose. Connection with a power greater than ourselves is the beginning of a spiritual awakening and the end of our suffering. We are finally ready to say, "I can't. You can. I think I'll let you." We become spiritually awake when we become willing to see things differently, and when our intention is to come from a place of love rather than fear.

I was an agnostic until my late thirties. I thought that maybe there was a God, maybe there wasn't, but we would never know. Early in my own spiritual journey, searching for answers, someone suggested that I put an extra "o" in the word God and to consider God a power for good and love. That made sense to me and is still a part of my belief.

Rabbi Harold Kushner writes, "For me, God is personal in the sense that He affects every individual differently. The rabbis of the Midrash said, 'God is like a mirror.' The mirror never changes but everyone who looks at it sees a different face." My friend Elaine said that perhaps God put a piece of himself in all of us and called it a soul.

There's a cute story about a professor who was an atheist, who was teaching a college class. He told the class that he was going to prove that there was no God.

He said, "God, if you are real, then I want you to knock me off this platform. I'll give you fifteen minutes!" Ten minutes went by. He kept taunting God, saying, "Here I am God. I'm still waiting." He was down to the last couple of minutes when a big, 240-pound football player happened to walk by the door and hear what the professor said.

The football player walked into the classroom in the last minute, walked up to the professor and hit him full force, sending him flying off the platform. The professor got up, obviously shaken and said, "Where did you come from, and why did you do that?"

The football player replied. "God was busy. He sent me!"

Buddhism teaches us that the root of suffering is craving or desire. When we want something to be different than it is, we suffer. We can actually live with a light heart when we gently accept our flaws, acknowledge that we are powerless over them and pray to have them removed and do our part to let them go.

Many times we don't know what steps to take to turn around our negative energy and feel lighter. Deep within us our hearts know, but we can't reach it because we are so blocked. Ask God for guidance before taking an action step. Go into your heart and connect with a power greater than yourself and trust that you will know what to do. But as the following shows, make sure you're listening for the answer.

> *The person whispered, "God, speak to me,"*
> *And a meadowlark sang.*
> *But, the person did not hear.*
> *So the person yelled, "God, speak to me,"*
> *And the thunder rolled across the sky.*
> *But, the person did not listen.*
> *The person looked around and said,*
> *"God let me see you,"*
> *And a star shone brightly.*
> *But the person did not see.*
> *And the person shouted, "God, show me a miracle,"*

And a life was born.

But, the person did not notice.

So, the person cried out in despair,

"Touch me, God, and let me know you are here."

Whereupon, God reached down and touched the person.

But, the person brushed the butterfly away . . .

and walked on.

—Author Unknown

This is a great reminder that God is always around us in the small and simple things that we take for granted. Don't miss out on a blessing because it isn't packaged the way that you expect.

Prayer

I have so much to do today that I shall
spend the first three hours in prayer.

—Martin Luther

What better way to start your day than by connecting with the energy and love of the God of your understanding. By simply having the intention to communicate with a power greater than yourself, your day begins on a positive and spiritual note. While most of us rarely have three hours to pray in the morning unless we are in a monastery, at a retreat or on vacation, a few moments is all we need to ask for strength and guidance.

Prayer and meditation are two ways in which we can connect with God or universal energy or our souls. Know that we are not alone, that there is a divine order in the universe, even though we can't always see it.

Many years ago, while still a doubter, a friend asked me, "If you were carrying a table and someone said they would help you by carrying one end, would you let her?"

"Of course!" I answered.

"Then why not let your higher power help you with your day?" continued my friend. Since then, because of countless instances of help I have received by inviting God into my day, my faith has deepened. I would not consider beginning my day without prayer. Now I simply ask for the knowledge of God's will for me and the power to carry it out. Madame Chiang Kai-shek said that she used to pray that God would do this or that. Later she prayed that God would make his will known to her.

Imagine you are in a cold room with an electric heater at one end. If you plug the heater in and turn it on in the morning, you will be warm all day. But the longer you wait to turn it on, the colder the room. And if you wait until the end of the day, you will have spent a day being cold unnecessarily.

It is often suggested that we pray harder. Emmet Fox suggests that instead we pray softly or gently. He says that the more quietly we pray, the better results we get. He has said to his congregation, "Pray with a feather—not with a pickaxe."

Morning prayer and meditation are, to me, similar connections with my higher self, my inner spirit, my higher power—God.

I become willing to open myself up to the deepest place within me and connect with all the energies of the universe, whatever they might be. I cannot define God and I truly have no idea who or what God is, or to whom or what I am praying. But I do know that there is power and energy in the universe and when I pray, I make that connection to that power and energy.

Mahatma Gandhi told us, "Prayer is the key of the morning and the bolt of the evening." Taking this time for ourselves, whether we take a few seconds or many minutes, doesn't matter. It is our quiet time, our personal time.

The evening is a good time to thank this higher power for our day, perhaps giving specific thanks for some particular thing, event or situation we experienced that day. Perhaps a prayer was answered or something went particularly well. Evening is a good time to review our day and, if need be, ask forgiveness for something we did about which we are not proud. Perhaps we did or said some thoughtless or careless thing, an intentional or unintentional harm done to someone.

And then it is time to go to sleep, resting in the knowledge that we have done the best we could with this day.

LETTING GO AFFIRMATION

God didn't promise days without pain,
laughter without sorrow, sun without rain, but
He did promise strength for the day, comfort
for the tears, and light for the way.

—AUTHOR UNKNOWN

Even though we can't always see it at the moment, no matter what we are going through, it will eventually lead us to peace and to purpose. What we might think is a disaster can bring us strength and wisdom.

When we see our world from our hearts, knowing God is in charge, we soften, connecting with a place so comforting, so loving, that a transformation takes place.

When I am going through a difficult time,
I place my hand over my heart, reminding myself of
the strength and love God gave me
to get through anything.

CHAPTER

6

Lives Transformed

When the founder of Hasidic Judaism, the great Rabbi Israel Shem Tov, saw misfortune threatening the Jews, it was his custom to go to a certain part of the forest to meditate. There he would light a fire, say a special prayer, and the miracle would be accomplished and the misfortune averted.

Later, when his disciple, the celebrated Maggid of Mezritch, had occasion, for the same reason, to intercede with heaven, he would go to the same place in the forest and say, "Master of the Universe, listen! I do not know how to light the fire, but I am still able to say the prayer," and again the miracle would be accomplished.

Still later, Rabbi Moshe-lieb of Sasov, in order to save his people once more, would go into the forest and say, "I do not know how to light the fire. I do not know the prayer, but I know the place and this must be sufficient." It was sufficient and the miracle was accomplished.

Then it fell to Rabbi Israel of Razhin to overcome misfortune. Sitting in his armchair, his head in his hands, he spoke to God. "I am unable to light the fire, and I do not know the prayer, and I cannot even find the place in the forest. All I can do is tell the story and this must be sufficient."

And it was sufficient. For God made man because he loves stories.

What the caterpillar calls the end of the world,
the master calls a butterfly.

—RICHARD BACH

S tories serve many purposes. They can entertain us, expand our imaginations, reduce our boredom and guide us. The importance of the stories you will read here serve these functions and much more. The following stories show us that we are not alone, that no matter what we have gone through, others have been there, too. They teach us that there is a way of getting to the other side of our pain. They inspire us, give us courage and most of all offer hope and comfort. We learn that sometimes when people go through their own dark night of the soul and they feel they cannot bear any more pain, they finally achieve a metamorphosis and find their wings.

We do not have a choice when a sudden tragedy or disappointment occurs, but we do have a choice about what we do with it. We can go through life saying, "Poor me, look what life, my mother, my father, did to me." Or we can rise above our situation and find a purpose in it, which can then be shared with others for their own growth.

Alcoholics Anonymous (AA) calls this "sharing our experience, strength and hope." I know of no greater example of people who have transformed a painful experience into help for others than recovering addicts. AA was founded by two men, "Dr. Bob" and "Bill W." After years of loss, shame and suffering, neither man could stop drinking, and they felt lost and hopeless. Bill Wilson, while hospitalized, cried out to God, "If there is a God, let him show himself! I am ready to do anything, anything!"

A great white light followed his plea. It seemed to Bill that he was on a mountain and there was a wind—not of air but of spirit. "And then it burst upon me," he went on to write, "and I was a free man. Slowly the ecstasy subsided. I lay on the bed, but now, for a time I was in another world, a new world of consciousness. All about me and through me there was a wonderful feeling of Presence, and I thought to myself, 'so this is the God of the preachers!' . . . In the wake of my spiritual experience there came a vision of a society of alcoholics. If each sufferer were to carry the news of the scientific hopelessness of alcoholism to each new prospect, he might be able to lay every newcomer wide open to a transforming spiritual experience. This concept proved to be the foundation of such success as AA has since achieved."[1] There are now over two million people worldwide in AA, and many more in Narcotics Anonymous (NA), Overeaters Anonymous (OA) and the many other programs modeled after AA.

Most of us do not have the kind of profound spiritual awakening that Bill W. did. Christina Baldwin puts this well when she writes, "Spirituality is the sacred center out of which all life comes, including Mondays and Tuesdays and rainy Saturday afternoons in all their mundane and glorious detail. . . . The spiritual journey is the soul's life comingling with ordinary life."

After having had a spiritual awakening, whether it be a sudden transformation, a gradual change or a new understanding, some of us find ourselves filled with a passion to tell our story and help others heal by our example. Other people gradually discover that they can turn their pain into purpose by working to change laws. The Smarts of Utah, who suffered so deeply when their daughter Elizabeth was kidnapped, fought hard to help establish the Amber Alert system so that missing children could be found more quickly. Other people find their experiences have changed their lives and were instrumental in making them better parents or better teachers or simply better people. Many have become more compassionate because they have a deeper understanding of suffering. Or they may have become more spiritual, having found a power greater than themselves, and are in turn more loving. They have learned that love is truly what we are here to share.

The following stories are from people who fit into all these categories. Their lives have been transformed by the actions they have taken. Their stories can be an inspiration to you as you find the courage to transform your own life. Many of the names are fictitious. Some are real. The stories are all real.

> *There is a crack in everything.*
> *That's how the light gets in.*
>
> —LEONARD COHEN

Breaking the Cycle of Abuse

L ooking back, Norma finally realized that it had been no mistake that she ended up in abusive relationships. She was the youngest of three children, and while her older sister seemed to do everything perfectly, Norma never did anything well enough to please her father. He always criticized her about everything she did, making her feel as if she could do nothing right. By the time Norma was in her teens, she became very rebellious and took up with the wrong crowd.

Physical abuse was added to her emotional abuse when she was sixteen years old and became involved with the wrong person. It took her two and a half years before she was finally able to break up with him, only to find someone else just like him right after.

Norma was a retail store manager and had been able to save a good amount of money through careful frugality. When she met her second boyfriend, she cleaned out her bank account for him, thinking he was everything she had been looking for, and they drove until all the money ran out, ending up in Jacksonville, Florida. It was here the physical abuse began. At first she ignored the warning signs, but he was into alcohol and drugs and soon ended up in jail.

The abuse continued even when Norma found out she was pregnant. When her boyfriend found out she was planning to leave him, he threatened he would come after her and harm her and her family. Norma was always afraid and came to believe him when he said that she was a nothing who could never make it on her own.

Even though she was pregnant, he once pushed her part of the way out of their car, and then pulled her back inside by her hair. The situation became worse and worse, and Ellen became more and more desperate, but she was still afraid to leave.

Finally, she gathered up the courage to call her mother, who wired her enough money to come home. As soon as her son was born, Norma moved in with her brother. She was so thrilled to have the baby, thinking that at last she would have someone who would love her.

Out from under the abuse, Norma was absolutely determined that her son would have a better life. She was able to qualify for welfare but had to sell her car to make ends meet. Fortunately, an opening came up in subsidized housing. She was able to work nights, and when her son was three years old, she was able to put him into day care. Wanting to do something good, considering her experiences and hoping to help others, she studied phlebotomy (the science of withdrawing blood) and has been able to make a good living for herself and her son.

Still, it took Norma two and a half years to let go of her anger. She still feels frightened at times when something triggers memories from the past, but it is getting better. There is a new man in her life who is gentle and kind and wonderful with her son. They're planning to marry soon. Once she was finally able to break the cycle of abuse, Norma began to have a more normal and fulfilling life.

Finding Her Purpose

orn in Brooklyn, New York, Arlene's parents were wonderful role models because they worked together to run the toy and bicycle business that supported the family. Her mother's lessons were that she could run both a house and a business well if only she were willing to roll up her sleeves and work hard. Her father taught by example that the quality of care given to customers is the mark of a good business owner.

Arlene's life took a different path than her parents, at least in her marriage. After thirteen years together, she and her husband divorced and went their separate ways. With the roots planted by her parents, Arlene decided that she, too, could keep her own home and live her life on her own terms. With only a high school diploma, Arlene decided that a government job would offer her the safety and security she needed right away. Starting at a low level, temporary job would give her a foot in the door. She believed that she could open the door wider by attending classes and by being willing to do jobs no one else wanted in order to earn advancement.

Arlene's early religious training had not encouraged her to seek a spiritual path or examine what it was she really believed in. Her government career, however, provided both the time and money for her to find and follow her true vocation—a spiritual way of life.

Among other things, Arlene studied the Ascended Masters, the teachings of Jesus Christ, Buddhism, the Kabbalah, Zen, Taoism, Native American spirituality, the Goddesses, Wiccan, and

New Age beliefs. When what she calls "the light" came to Arlene, it was the simple, powerful instruction that people should love one another and be careful to do no harm.

Arlene had always followed her intuitive feelings about what changes she should make as she moved through life. On the edge of taking an advancement at work, she suddenly knew that, even though she was only eight years short of retirement, she had completed her time with the government.

She knew then that her new work would be teaching others about her twenty-year journey in the spirit, to help them lift any barriers in their way of finding their own inner wisdom, self-healing, empowerment and self-love, and to teach them that in a loving universe, all that is required is to ask and believe.

Having found her purpose, Arlene realized that she needed to return to her strong roots—modeling herself on the parents who taught her to run a store—and create a sacred space that she now calls a teaching/healing place.

As she had always done, Arlene prepared for her new job by reading books on how to start a business, how to form a corporation and what licenses were required. She didn't listen to naysayers and forged ahead with her plans. On May 1, 1996, she opened Woman's Wish in quaint Occoquan, Virginia, a bookstore and gift shop for women. It reflects Arlene's special style and is a place where she holds circles and workshops for empowering women on all subjects, beliefs and ideas.

Following a Spiritual Path

O ver the years, all the trauma that Samantha—better known as Sam—went through expressed itself in her body. At different times she came down with chronic fibromyalgia, was treated for throat cancer and then had to have an aneurysm (which could have burst at any moment) removed from her esophagus.

Sam can trace many of her problems back to her divorce from her husband. He had become so mentally abusive that she had no choice but to end their marriage. She definitely believes that her daughter Joie's troubles began then, because that is when she started hanging out with people who lived wildly and drew her daughter in with them. Tragically, her gentle, loving, twenty-year-old daughter died in an accident caused by one of those "friends," who was driving drunk while Joie was a passenger in the car.

Sam had named her daughter Joie because it is French for "joy," Sam's predominant emotion when she brought her little adopted daughter home for the first time. She didn't have the gift of giving birth to her, but later, she experienced the pain of Joie's birth into eternal life. She sees both of these Joie's as having been her privilege to love.

It was because of Joie's death that Sam decided to return to school to become a psychotherapist. She knew she couldn't waste her daughter's death and had to find a way to use it in a positive way. Sam recalls the three years her training took as being "gruelingly difficult." Unfortunately, it was also during that time that

Sam was developing throat cancer.

After graduation she took a month-long spiritual retreat to the Southwest, where she stayed in a convent, practiced silence and received spiritual direction.

A year or so after her return, when she was diagnosed with the cancer and had been treated for it, Sam went on a six-month trip with the hope of finding her spiritual home. She worked hard on her spirituality, drawing on both prayer and meditation. All the while she lived "out of her car" and stayed in places that presented themselves as having something to offer her in her search—that is, convents, monasteries, ashrams, a tree house, an adobe bungalow, a trailer, etc. When the journey was over, Sam ended up back where she started as a child, on Cape Cod in Massachusetts.

Before having her second surgery, this time for her aneurysm, Sam connected with a therapist named Peggy Huddleston with the hope of learning how to remove her fears. Peggy used a model for healing that Sam later drew upon herself to help others going through fear and stress. Both women believe that relieving stress is a path to healing for people facing traumas. It is the method Sam believes in and practices with her clients today. She feels that this work is what she was born to do and what she was inspired to do by her daughter's death.

Today, Sam is happy, healthy and living with her new husband who is a treasure in her life.

My gratitude speaks when I
share it with others.

—Scott H.

Gratitude

S cott didn't grow up in a family where alcohol or drugs were a problem. Yet he had been an addict for as far back as he could remember. Scott felt that he never had enough of anything. He wasn't tall enough, smart enough, good looking enough, fast enough or friendly enough. You name it, Scott never felt that he had enough of it.

He so desperately wanted to fit in that he did everything he could to gain acceptance. All he needed was a cheering section and he would perform. People would say, "Oh, look at Scott, isn't he cute?" and he would feel good, not believing what they said a moment later.

He was introduced to his first addictive substance at seven when he drank an apricot sour and passed out. When he was eleven years old he was experimenting with light alcohol, by twelve it was marijuana, and by thirteen or fourteen he was stealing Valium from his mother and taking with hot tea so he could, in his words, "get off quicker." Only under the influence of a mind-altering substance did Scott feel "good enough." It gave him a false sense of security, but only for as long as the effects lasted.

Scott used drugs throughout junior high school and high school—before, after and during each school day. He spent the first year and a half of his time in college partying and was caught cheating on an exam. He was told that if that ever happened again he would be expelled. It did. And he was.

When he left school, Scott went home to a wonderful opportunity to work in his family business. He was given the chance to travel and grow with it, and he did very well. At first he did so well he was able to afford his drug habit, and he moved to New Jersey, near the George Washington Bridge, from which he could get to Manhattan and his drugs easily. It all seemed perfect to him, but not to others. From time to time over the next five years, Scott's family would have sit-down sessions with him, telling him that he had to get it together and carry his weight. They all had family obligations and were worried about losing everything. Soon it became so bad that they threatened he would have to leave if he didn't go to therapy for drug addiction and stop using.

Scott promised he would go for help, and he did. But he went to his sessions late and left early. He was so sure and prideful and stubborn, and he never asked anyone for help.

During this time, the woman that he had been in a relationship with walked out on him. Not being able to handle the feelings, Scott picked up a sixteen-ounce bottle of beer. He planned to go back to his group the next day. However, as usually happens, his addictions took over, and Scott went on a long and painful three-day trip into his addiction, in which he ended up hurting people who were close to him. He was floundering, and his life was going nowhere. Still, he remained in complete denial that drugs and alcohol were his problem. He became so desperate, and reached such a bottom, that he ended up breaking into houses and stealing from his neighbors, his family, his friends and even his customers to feed his addiction.

At the end of this terrible time, Scott was thirty-four years old and weighed only ninety-six pounds. He had gone from being a man who wore expensive shoes and Armani suits to ending up in the inner city without a dime in his pockets.

He remembers that it was a Sunday, October 26, 1988. He could barely walk and had been evicted from where he was staying because he hadn't paid his rent. He would have to walk over the George Washington Bridge to get back to his family. Along the way he begged for money for the train.

Scott's brother opened his heart to him, letting him stay at his house, and took him to a Narcotics Anonymous meeting that called itself, appropriately, the Emergency Room.

The people at the meeting were wonderful to Scott. They gave him a list of recovery meetings, put their phone numbers on it, asked for his number and invited him out for coffee. They told him to call if he needed a ride or if he felt like using.

One person nominated Scott to make coffee and that made him very angry at first. He thought the person was trying to embarrass him or punish him until he found out that the man was doing for Scott that which had been done for him. It was a way of giving Scott a place in the community.

Scott hadn't opened his mail in eighteen months. When he did, he discovered to his horror that he was $48,000 in debt. He had been sleeping on a cot with no sheets and thought, "How can

I be responsible for making this group's coffee if I can't even be responsible for myself?" But he tried to make it anyway. It was terrible, but it resulted in his making a lot of friends.

He was told that it's all right to make a mistake in recovery, that he should be grateful that he kept on trying. He was told that recovery had very little to do with him and everything to do with God and the people God put into his life.

Scott became grateful for the people in the fellowship because they were always there for him. It was a tremendous struggle in the beginning and he wanted to use drugs all the time. Instead, he went to meetings. He made coffee. He shared.

Something magical began to happen because he stayed close to his program. He finally asked someone to be his sponsor, which is a guide or a mentor in twelve-step programs. His sponsor encouraged him to do service work, so he began to carry the message of hope to institutions and hospitals to addicts who still suffered. Scott began feeling good about sharing his message because it was given to people who didn't have hope from someone (himself) who now *did* have hope. And he came to see that service work was selfish. It made him feel good. He was getting something back for doing the right thing for the right reasons. Scott got involved, and he gave away freely what was given to him. He learned that with freedom comes responsibility.

Scott says that pain has been a great motivating force in his recovery. It hasn't been an easy road for him, but it has been a simple road. He tries to be the best person he can be. Through the steps of recovery, he has been able to make a miraculous transformation, and he has come to believe in spiritual principles. He has learned that acceptance, hope, faith, honesty, humility, perseverance and spirituality are the answers.

Today he has many good people in his life. Over the years he lost his father, went through the breakup of relationships and stayed clean. He says," If I'm willing to take the next step, God has always put the path beneath my feet."

Still, throughout the years, Scott continued to seek something outside himself to fill the void on the inside. He went through a very painful time with sexual addiction. When he was eight years clean and sober, he wanted to kill himself over it because he was feeling so very lonely, unlovable and unable to love. His sponsor told him to abstain from relationships and sex, get back to more meetings and make a commitment to service.

Scott said this was like going through detox all over again. It was like detoxifying from neediness. He lived through anxiety attacks, managing somehow to "walk through them." He decided it was more important to be the right person than to meet the right person.

Finally, God put someone in his life when he wasn't even looking for her. He was able to build a relationship with a woman who turned out to be his best friend, companion, confidante and lover.

One day, Scott started casually e-mailing meditations of the day to a few of his friends—who forwarded them to a few of their friends, who forwarded them to a few of theirs, and so on. Soon others began to send poems and inspirational stories to Scott.

The outcome has been *12-Step Soul Food for the Spirit,* an e-mail newsletter now in its fifth year and received by 6,500 recovering people in sixty-four countries. It connects people to meetings all over the world.

Scott's belief about addiction is that "there's a God-shaped hole that only God can fill. We used to fill it with gambling, overeating, alcohol, drugs. Now it's filled with God. The law of the spirit is overflowing with abundance."

Finding Inspiration

Barbara is one of those courageous women who dared to go back to school when she was forty-seven years old. Life had been very difficult and often painful for her up until then. She had four children, the first when she was a teenager and the fourth when she was twenty-six years old. For years she supported them alone as a single mom. She married for the second time later in life and had another child when she was forty-three.

At the age of forty-seven, Barbara had an exciting opportunity to go to college, something that she could never before fit into her life. It was an alternative college that gave credit for one's life experiences, so she was able to finish undergraduate school quickly and go on to graduate school. Unfortunately, her new marriage was in trouble, and being in school full-time was overwhelming. At one point, she felt she needed to take a break. A friend very wisely said,

"Barbara, there will always be overwhelming circumstances in life. If you stop now, you won't come back." Barbara knew she was right and stayed in school. That became one of the most important decisions she ever made in her life.

Sandy Bierig had a small grant for her alcohol and drug abuse treatment program at the Massachusetts Women's Correctional Institution in Framingham, and she needed someone to head a peer support program she had started in the prison. She felt Barbara was perfect for the job.

Barbara had been interested in the life and work of Mother Teresa since she had read a book about her titled *Something Beautiful for God,* by Father Varghese Parappuram. The title had been suggested by Mother Teresa herself with the explanation that, "Every day, on awakening, my desire and my enthusiasm is that I must do something beautiful today for God. What is there that I can do better for God than to console the distressed, wipe away the tears of those who weep, be a refuge to the abandoned, and pour love into the hearts of the unloved?" Mother Teresa had believed that these are the things that are beautiful in the sight of God.

Barbara was awed by the courage and perseverance of this humble woman, but she had no idea how this woman would continue to inspire her life later.

Mother Teresa had worked with the poorest of the poor in India. Barbara realized she could work with the poorest of the poor in so many ways right here in her own community.

"The lives of the women in the prison had been filled with such deprivation. They had suffered so much pain and difficulty. I knew it wasn't my job to change all their lives. I could only be with the people that were placed in my path on any given day and love them just as they were. Mother Teresa spoke about this same thing in her own work. In order to prevent burnout and keep from being completely overwhelmed with the enormity of what was around her in terms of human suffering, she had to focus on just one person at a time, just the one in front of her.

"I could not cure these women of their drug addiction or alcoholism. I couldn't take away their poverty. I could not give them back their lost children. I could only assist them on their journey within, to find the beauty of their own souls."

One of the highlights of Barbara's life began in June 1988 with a flurry of excitement around prison security because a notable person would be visiting the institution. This time, Barbara was to receive a very huge gift. She was asked to come in on a Sunday and take pictures in the prison while Mother Teresa visited.

The day came and there was a lot of excitement. There was a group of people, including prison officials, a state representative and Barbara, who walked around the prison with Mother Teresa.

The power being generated during that visit was profound. Tiny and delicate looking for such a strong, hard-driving woman, Mother Teresa always had a slight smile on her face as she moved along through the halls and among the inmates and the staff. Barbara thought she looked as if she had a little secret.

She spoke to the women very simply about just loving one another, giving a smile to all in their paths as a way of carrying God's love. It was not a message that said to just grin and bear their pain. Instead, she was teaching them how to pass on God's love, keeping some for themselves. As Barbara listened to her she became aware that there were tears running down her face and the faces of the others around her.

"The unique part of that experience was that I knew in those moments that the power was not coming from her. She was not the power. She was just simply a vessel who was so clear, so free, that the power who I call God was coming through her with so little obstruction that you could feel the energy. It was the most powerful experience I ever had in my life. This was a human being who was free of fear and ego. That is why she was able to do what she did and why people reacted to her the way they did. She loved every human being she spoke to because they were God in disguise to her.

"When I had an opportunity to speak one-on-one with her, she looked right into my eyes, and I knew I was the only person on earth to her in that moment. I knew that I had experienced something in my life that would be part of me always, something that had peeled away more of the layers that would have blocked the connection between me and others, and me and God.

"The message for me in all of that is that the joy and the purpose in our lives is in a very deep place and becomes strengthened by life and the experiences to which we say yes. Mother Teresa's state of being was tremendously evolved, and yet she believed that the same spirit that was in her is in all of us."

Although she has her own therapeutic practice today, Barbara continues to pray for the women in the prison, asking that all who pass through that dark time of their lives may find the light and the freedom that is possible for all of us.

"I will always be grateful for the wounds I've had in my life. They allow me to maintain the compassion and understanding that otherwise may have eluded me."

In Spite of the Pain

Max Springer is a wonderful example of a person who has never forgotten his pain, but has been able to find a greater purpose in his problems. When Max was only ten years old, Germany was already rapidly swallowing Eastern Europe. His parents knew that they had to get their children to safety, and his father was somehow able to make arrangements for Max to leave his family and his country and go to England, which had agreed to accept 10,000 child refugees. It took more than a year to arrange because his father had lost his citizenship papers, but Max finally left with Kinder Transport, a program set up to help Jewish children from Germany, Austria and Czechoslovakia flee to safer countries during World War II. The majority of the children who left never again saw their parents because most of them died in concentration camps such as Auschwitz.

Max's older brother had fortunately been sent to America in August of 1938, and Max went to live with distant cousins in

London where he didn't really know anyone and didn't speak the language. His exile lasted from June 1939 to May 1946, when he was seventeen years old.

Miraculously, Max's mother was able to stay in their apartment in Germany. He was able to talk to her by phone weekly up until March 1943, when she was taken and sent to Auschwitz. After the war, Max found out from the Red Cross that, while his mother had been put on board a train for the concentration camp, she had never actually arrived there. Because it was such a brutal trip, many people on the trains died en route to the camps. Max's mother was among them.

Max's father had been sent to a concentration camp in 1940. He spent five years and eight months in different camps, the last being Bergen-Belsen, and somehow managed to survive. He was released in May 1945 and went to America in December 1946, where he and Max were reunited.

While he was interned, Max's father kept a careful diary of the painful story of his time in the camps and saved it for his children to read, so that they would know the horrors of the Holocaust. By the time he came to the United States, Max's father was emotionally dead. But his children and grandchildren all know what happened in the camps because he made it come to life for them.

Having seen it through his father's eyes, Max believes that those who did survive the concentration camps were able to do it for two reasons: 95 percent luck and 5 percent a strong instinct to live.

One of the stories his father told was that he stopped eating bread once for a week and survived by eating just grass. He did this to test himself to see if he had the ability to endure outside the camp, in case he was ever able to escape.

As he grew older, Max's loneliness was palpable. He was so damaged when he emigrated to America that he rarely spoke until eleven years later, when he met his future wife.

Although not yet a citizen, Max was drafted into the army during the Korean War. When he came back, he was able to use the GI Bill of Rights to attend the architectural department of the Institute of Design and Construction where he learned to be a draftsman. Although not able to actually go to college because his formal education had ended when he was only fourteen years old, Max worked with brilliant people. He considers his contact with these people to be his college education—along with the enormous amount of reading he has done throughout his life.

Active in the Young Zionist's Movement in his twenties, Max intended eventually to emigrate to Israel to live and work in a kibbutz. Before leaving, however, as fate would have it, Max decided to attend a Young Adults' campout founded by the United Jewish Appeal. It was there that he met the woman he would marry and whom he credits with opening him up to the world. It was love at first sight. They both knew right away that they would be married, and just a few months later, they were.

Now, Max is grateful that his ability to disassociate from the reality of his life during the early years helped to wipe out much of its painful details. Consequently, he only remembers some of the awful times that he went through. Max says there are three kinds of Holocaust survivors: people so traumatized that they never speak of their trauma and they live in misery; people who remember, put it behind them and go on with their lives; and people who remember, go on with their lives and become a driving force to help people remember the Holocaust.

If that is true, Max fits into the third category. He still speaks in public schools whenever he can, to keep the message alive, so that what happened to the six million Jews and five million Christians will never happen again.

While Max still lives with his memories, he says, "It's something that I just carry with me. I live with it all along, but time teaches you how to deal with it. These things don't just go away, but you don't dwell on them. You do enjoy things in life. I love music, the museums, travel. I love my family."

Max knows how lucky he was to marry someone who was upbeat and positive. She has made all the difference in his life. His wife doesn't take all of the credit, however. She told me that Max has been able to survive and live a basically normal life because he had the love and care of his family in his early years and love continues to carry him through.

In spite of his tremendous losses, Max chooses to live his life in a manner intended to bring lightness to others—the lightness of which he was robbed. This takes an extraordinarily willing attitude.

Moving Forward Again

I n January 1993, I had a healthy and strong husband of five years, a four-year-old daughter, a job at a wonderful elementary school with a great principal and faculty. We had bought a house two years earlier. One day my husband, Jules, came home and complained about a sensation in his chest. He remarked about it for a couple of weeks and then made an appointment at our HMO. He went there one evening after work and they took an X ray. The doctor told him he was right about feeling as though there was something in there, because he could see a tumor the size of a grapefruit!

"When Jules came home and told me the news I felt like a bomb had been dropped. I felt that our lives would never be the same again. I was scared. We were scared. Jules had buried his first wife due to breast cancer six years earlier, and he had taken care of her for the two and a half years before her death.

"Within days we were at Brigham and Women's Hospital in Boston, seeing several leading oncologists.

"They looked at this six-foot, three-and-a-half-inch handsome man in great running shape, and then they looked at the X ray—and they were baffled. They said that maybe one hundred people in medical history have had what Jules had. It was a connective tissue cancer, not in the extremities where it's usually found, but in his lung. They admitted that they had no idea what to do, and they left us in a room, alone, to begin making plans for Jules' death. We cried together, and then we called our families right then and there.

"Meanwhile, a Dr. Sugarbaker, a famous surgeon, came on to consult, and he said he wanted to remove Jules' entire right lung. Jules agreed to the surgery, and I remember thinking how brave he was to choose to do this. How determined he was to try something so huge to extend his life. In February he had the surgery, which left a scar from his breast bone in the front all the way around to his spine in the back.

"I remember being given the "Footprints" passage then and reading it out loud for the very first time in the ICU with Jules. That passage was one of many things that helped me through that very rough time.

"In fact, I will tell you the only time I ever felt comfort was when I was in prayer to *G-d*.* I'd start with the *Shema* in Hebrew, and then I'd pray in English. This is a special prayer that Jews are obligated to recite in the morning and in the evening. It is both an affirmation of Judaisim and a declaration of faith in God. They were the only times I ever felt comfort during those rough times.

"The cloud of impending doom continued to hang over us from January to August 20, 1993, when Jules died in our home. He had turned forty-one on August 15, and Sara would turn five on August 30.

"Our rabbi was a g-dsend this whole time. He answered all of our questions, including all of Sara's, and came around often.

---

*Among observant Jews, it is forbidden to erase or deface the written name of God. A dash is inserted in the middle of God's name so the word can be erased or the paper it's written on can be discarded.

Sometimes the answer to our questions was, "We really don't know; however, this is what we think. . . ."

"After the *shiva* period, which is the seven-day mourning period observed by the immediate family of the deceased, the rabbi suggested Sara and I go out the front door of our home and walk around the block in a clockwise direction to experience moving forward in life. I completely absorbed myself in Jewish studies of death, dying, mourning and grieving. I knew that there were lots of writing and teachings about the subject, and I knew nothing. I looked toward my religion for information and comfort. I trusted in the experience, customs, beliefs and knowledge of my very old religion—Judaism. It's the only way I made it through that awful time.

"Gratefully, my love for my daughter was another very important motivator for me—through Jules' illness and death—encouraging me to experience, learn and grow. That June of 1993, I asked for help in order to get myself together for talking with Sara, and I was sent to a wonderful woman who happened to be a child psychiatrist. As it turned out, Sara never went, only I did. The doctor was wonderful. She kept me focused on simplicity and honesty and guided me in the task of sharing Jules' impending death with Sara. I read as many books as I could during that period on death, dying and grieving.

"I believe that the soul lives on after death and that every time I speak the name of my loved ones or think about them, I set their souls alight. The memory of our loved ones is truly a blessing, and I want only to be worthy of their memory.

"About three years ago, I found again and listened to the tape Jules had recorded for me right before we married, which he played for me when we were at Machu Pichu in Peru for our honeymoon. It says, 'So, hold me tight, hold me tight in your memory . . . in your vision . . . and when you're thinking of me, I'm thinking of you . . . and I'll see you soon my love . . . Bye.' Isn't that nice? Listening to it lifted my heart. It made me wonder if our path was already set out or carved by fate.

"Sara wasn't quite five at the time of her father's death. He used to pretend that he was going to go into space. She didn't realize for a long time that he wasn't coming back."

Now Sara knows that her mom stayed strong and made sure they got through his loss. Sara knows, too, that she is stronger because of it, although her friends can't see the changes in her because the changes are on the inside. She also knows that she cherishes her mom more now.

Guilt, shame and blame drain us of
our strength and separate us from our reservoirs
of strength within us, so that they may go
untapped for years or perhaps
our entire lives.

—DR. BERNIE SIEGAL

Rainbow Story

Debra spent many years of her life lost in guilt, shame, depression and low self-esteem. She was unhappy most of the time, feeling as if she had lost a part of herself. Her parents were divorced when she was around five. Right before they separated, they had a big argument. Her father became violent, and her mother took Debra and walked out, never to return.

Subsequently, her mother became negative, angry, violent and hateful. Today, Debra knows she needed psychiatric help then but never got it. Alone, it was obvious that her mother didn't know how to be a parent. She was a martyr who continually made Debra feel guilty by saying, "After everything I've done for you . . ." So, Debra was turned into a mini-mother, required to parent her own mother. In spite of that, Debra's mother dominated and manipulated her until she died, when Debra was thirty-five.

Somewhere between the ages of five and six, Debra became prey to the sexual abuse of her next-door neighbor. His job was to water the plants in the local cemetery, and he would take little kids with him on his trips. Debra went with him several times. Her mother, becoming a little suspicious, asked if anything was going on, but Debra never told her because she was afraid her mother would kill her. In fact, she never told anyone until forty-five years later.

Debra grew up thinking she had no choices, an idea that all the adults in her life reinforced. She couldn't see that she had any options. She became depressed and suicidal when she wanted to leave school and her mother said no.

Many years later, when she was around forty-five years old and having an intimate moment with her husband, Debra suddenly heard a voice that sounded as if it were coming from someone in the room. "Cut it out, or you'll get hit," the voice said. Debra, completely unaware of why, was instantly filled with feelings of shame and guilt. She wanted to tell her husband about the experience, but was afraid he wouldn't understand.

When Debra did finally go into therapy, it was because she was having difficulty with a new boss. She just couldn't bring herself to fire someone as the boss directed. She thought the therapy would be only for a short period, but it was the beginning of a real period of change, growth and recovery for her.

One of the things she discovered was that she had absolutely no sense of personal boundaries. All her boundaries had been violated throughout her life by a series of authority figures, starting with her mother. Unwittingly, Debra had become very good at hiding herself and how she felt about things, even *from* herself.

Debra also found that she had sensations, not memories. Over the years, she had learned to disassociate from what was happening to her by canceling out the actual events that triggered them in her memory. But her body maintained its connection to them by remembering the sensations they evoked. At one point in her therapy, she became suicidal. One day, motivated by emotional pain, Debra drove out to the beach, pulled by the desire to walk out into the sea and swim and swim until she became too tired to swim back to shore, and then drown.

Through a huge effort, she pulled herself away from the beach, and these thoughts and drove directly to her therapist, who called Debra's husband. The therapist agreed not to send Debra to the hospital if she promised to tell her husband what had been going on. Debra felt an overwhelming panic, as if she were being torn apart. "They are going to find out," she worried. "They are going to take me away." She had been told early that no one would believe her abuse story and that if she told anyone, she would disappear like her father had.

Instead, she learned to confront her demons through various methods, including talk therapy, EMDR (tapping), journaling, massage, affirmations, meditation and spiritual involvement. At some point, Debra could finally tell her story but remain emotionally detached from it. And soon she found an inner strength she didn't know she had.

She remembers that it was a Memorial Day when she was first able to detach from a panic attack. It had always been a big and painful ordeal to decorate her mother's grave. Her husband offered to do it for her this time, joking that her mother would get her for not doing it herself. Debra said, "I don't care!" and knew she meant it.

Church was important while Debra was growing up, partly because she was forced to go. But God wasn't welcoming and loving back then. Many years later, when she was eight months into treatment, she had a spiritual epiphany. Debra was in the mountains during the fall foliage season. She walked around the lake she had stopped at and climbed up on a bench to view Mt. Washington. She had what she called a real "God-spoke-to-me" moment.

"I looked up and it was late enough in the year so that there was snow on Mt. Washington. Above me were beautiful trees in full color. Above the trees I could see another layer, a tundra . . . full of ice and snow. I could see how isolated and lonely it must be at the top of the mountain and how much warmer it was down below the tree line, where it was bright and colorful. Suddenly, I felt compelled to recite the Twenty-First Psalm. When I couldn't remember all the words, I burst out sobbing.

"God was speaking to me, telling me that I didn't have to go through my pain alone, that there were many people who were warm and delightful. Two weeks later I declared, 'I have to go to church today.' People in the church had been praying for me and were thrilled that I was there.

"It was Good Friday, and the sermon reminded me how cruel the crucifixion had been. His willingness to suffer that death had been his testimony of love. I had been seeking love for so long that

I felt completely relieved of my pain and grief. It was like finding the Holy Grail. This love had been there all along. Now, no matter what happens in the real world, I know I am loved, and I'm all right. I am contented most of the time. Now my heart is light.

"A few years ago, I opened a gift shop on Cape Cod as a celebration of my inner spirit. I named it Debra Ann's Rainbow in honor of that inner spirit, my inner child, that kept me alive all these years. I have a lot fun with the store. I feel that it is a wonderful way to connect with people from all over, and I offer them something with which to remember me and their time at the beach.

"As I was facing fifty, I was terrified that I would die. Now, when I do die, I will know that I have truly lived."

Reaching Out to Others

A week before Linda's brother turned eighteen, she had the same dream every night. She dreamt that her mother would die, and she would finish up her journey through life with her father.

Her mother gave a wonderful eighteenth birthday party for her brother (Linda was fourteen years old). At that time, eighteen was the legal age for drinking in New York, so there was beer at the party. At the end of the evening, her father was concerned about the boys who had been drinking, so he, her brothers and a few of their friends, went out across the street to each car to make sure that the drivers weren't drunk.

Linda's mother went out also, but just before she went through the door, she and Linda looked at each other briefly. In that brief second Linda felt as if her mother had given her something important, although she didn't know what it was at the time.

Outside, Linda's mother and her grandmother were standing on the street, watching and waiting for her brother and two of his friends, who were coming back across the road toward them. From the corner of her eye Linda saw a car come up the road and, as she remembers it, everything went into slow motion. The car hit all six people. Her mother was the one who actually went under the car. Everyone else was thrown aside. Many years later, Linda was able to recall that she had physically lifted her brother out of the road.

Three ambulances came and took everyone away. Linda went to her sister-in-law's house and waited until her older brother finally came to get her and take her to the hospital. By the time she arrived her mother had died. She was the only one who was killed. Everyone else was only injured.

Her grandmother and the rest of the family were horrified. They didn't know how to tell her dad, who also had been admitted to the hospital. Linda said she would tell him. It was a terrible, terrible thing for a fourteen-year-old to have to do.

After the accident, two kids jumped into their car and chased the car that had caused the accident. The driver turned out to be drunk. At that time there were no good laws about drunk driving. The family did take the driver to civil court several years later but lost the case. Linda remembers her dad saying to the driver, "We forgave you for our sakes. However, you never even made a phone call, you never even sent a flower, and that's something you'll live with for the rest of your life."

The loss of her mother changed Linda's life forever. As a very young girl she had to take on two or three jobs to help her dad. She put herself through college and went through a lot of hard challenges. That's not to say she didn't have fun as a teenager, but it was very difficult as well.

Linda realized that her mother had given her a lot of her strength and psychic abilities when she left, and that's something she'll never forget. It gave her courage.

Linda was faced with a lot of choices in her life. As a young girl, she could have gotten into drugs, but she said no. She made a different choice. She decided that she needed to "take her mom along with her," in her mind, so that her mom could have the journey that she missed because of her early death. Everything Linda chose to do in her life—get a good education, make a good marriage, have children, give back to the community—was done with her mother in mind, so that her mom could share it with her.

Linda's father died when she was twenty-seven years old, and that was really hard. She said to herself, "Okay, now you're really on your own!"

In her thirties, Linda started to experience some anxiety. She went to a counselor who diagnosed her with post-traumatic stress disorder. He said that what she had seen as a child was horrifying. And the only way she got through it was that she was always able to talk about it. And accept it. She continued to see the counselor for a few years until her symptoms passed.

When her children turned fourteen, Linda became aware that she had had a mother only until she was fourteen. Now what would she do? How would she know how to mother her children? But she was lucky to have a lot of women in her life, good friends of hers from high school, whose mothers had been surrogate parents for Linda. She learned so much from each and every one of them and from her mother-in-law. They taught her how to be a mom. She was also lucky to have a large extended family, and even though they had divorced, she stayed close to her ex-husband's family.

Linda knew she needed to work with other people. And through her psychic abilities and her own sense of understanding and wisdom, she is always helping other people. Linda feels that we learn so much about ourselves when we give to others. She counsels others because of her horrific experiences. Every time she hears of someone who has lost a child or lost a parent, she tries to take the time to tell them that they will survive.

Linda knows that it is important to be strong, but she also realizes that it's not what happens on your journey in life, but what you do with it.

Never does the human soul appear
so strong as when it foregoes revenge, and
dares forgive an injury.

—E. H. CHAPIN

Spiritual Coins

Ann spent wonderful visits with her daughter when Sally came to her home. They walked and had long talks, and it was a very nurturing time for their relationship. Later, Ann was to say that those visits were a treasure, a godsend.

Sally, a thirty-three-year-old mother of three children, had separated from her husband a few weeks before one of her planned visits to her mother. While Sally was at her own home, she had been sitting on the steps outside when a young women came by, asking if there were any apartments to rent in the neighborhood.

The woman also asked if Sally had any old clothes for her children. She was told to come back in a week and Sally would have some clothes for her. Unexpectedly, a few days later, while Sally was having lunch in a restaurant, the same woman came in and sat with her.

A week later, Sally's twenty-one-year-old brother was planning to spend the weekend with her while her three children were spending the weekend with their father. He arrived to find a horrible scene. He found his murdered sister's body. Blood was everywhere.

Ann received the call and immediately went to Sally's house. At first the police wouldn't even let her in. Ann kept repeating to herself, "I'll be okay. I'll be okay," and to her daughter, "You're in a better place." She sat on the steps of the house and wouldn't go away until the police talked to her.

She insisted on cleaning the house herself and finally convinced the police to let her do it. It was very painful, a "heavy" experience as she describes it, but she had to do it. It was like the last thing she could really do for her daughter.

The ensuing six months to a year were very difficult. Ann was preoccupied with the trial of her daughter's murderer and she worried about her sons. She would tell herself that she had to get on with her life but she had headaches and ground her teeth at night to such an extent that she had to see a dentist to save her teeth.

Sally's younger brother was never the same after his sister was killed. Since she was twelve years his senior, Sally had been like a mother to him, and they were very close. He fell apart, suddenly breaking off his engagement to a girl he really loved and then joining the Marines.

Only through prayer and her strong faith was Ann able to get through this time. She knew she had a pocketful of spiritual coins because of her faith in the past that she used as she worked on pulling the family back together. After a year of being locked inside of herself with her pain, Ann was finally able to begin to throw off the mantle of grief that had engulfed her. She took walks on the beach again and was able to begin to see all the good things that she had in her life.

Ann was blessed to have had wonderful, spiritual parents, and she and her daughter had been great friends because they liked each other. She was lucky enough to have never had serious financial problems, and she had good friends and the ability to bond with people. Her faith was a wonderful comfort to her, and she could see it growing stronger and stronger within her. When she added her assets and subtracted her deficits, she saw that she came out far ahead on the asset side.

As a further aid to healing, Ann began to go to Compassionate Friends, a support group where parents and siblings who have lost children and brothers and sisters meet once a month for support. Soon she started her own group for parents of murdered children. As part of her service, she would always go to court to support a parent when needed.

Ann went to court every day during her daughter's murder trial. Every day she saw the mother of the woman who was accused of murdering her daughter. Every day that mother had to see her eighteen-year-old daughter, whom she loved, shackled in chains and brought into the courtroom.

One day the two mothers met in the ladies room. To her amazement, Ann was able to feel pity for her. She had two little statues of the Blessed Virgin in the pocket of the coat she had on, which she hadn't worn in years. She gave the woman one of the little statuettes. The woman said, "Thank you. I had an aunt who was a nun and she gave me the same statue years ago. Now, I feel I have it back."

Ann told her that this mother, the Blessed Virgin of the statue, went through a terrible time when she lost her Son, and maybe she could help them through this.

"I don't know where the words came from. I felt cleared. A little part of me was healed."

It came out in the trial that Ann's daughter, Sally, had filled two pillowcases of children's clothes for her killer. After she killed Sally, the woman not only took the clothes but also Sally's jewelry and emptied her medicine chest.

The woman was convicted and sentenced to life without parole. She later appealed, and Ann had to sit through the terrible ordeal of a four-week trial again, but the verdict stood.

Ann believes your soul is rewarded in the afterlife. "Whether I'm right or I'm wrong in everything I believe doesn't matter," she said. "It gives me great happiness. The Lord has directed my life. Nothing is an accident. After the first year I was given the gift of being able to let go of my pain and anger."

Ann believes strength comes through struggle.

The Heart-Lightening Process
Step 6:

TAKE ACTION

> *My heart is to be my workshop,*
> *my laboratory, my great enterprise, and love is*
> *to be my contribution to humanity.*
>
> —EMMET FOX

Perhaps we are holding on to a resentment. We have stopped, felt it and accepted it. Our intention is to feel joy, and now we know that when our hearts are blocked with negative emotions, joy can't be felt. We've also learned by now that we have the power to change how we feel. A spiritual action step might be to forgive the person you feel has wronged you. This does not mean you must accept what this person has done. It simply means that you are not willing to carry negative energy with you any longer, and you are willing to let it go. Karen Casey writes, "When we forgive others we accelerate our growth. We see opportunities that resentments blocked." Another action step is expressing how you are feeling. When we keep whatever is bothering us inside, joy and peace are impossible.

The Importance of Expressing Ourselves

> *The doors we open and close today*
> *decide the lives we live.*
>
> —FLORA WHITTEMORE

It is essential that we do not keep our feelings locked up inside ourselves. When we do this we are closing our hearts, blocking any possibility of feeling joy and other higher energy feelings. Even if we are not aware of it, and feelings are at a subconscious level, our hearts have no opportunity to be open. Old resentments, feelings of low self-worth, guilt and shame, block any chance we might have of living as light as a feather. Whatever is going on inside us needs to be expressed or it will damage us mentally, physically and spiritually.

In Latin, the prefix "ex" means "out." The word "express," therefore means to "press out," or communicate. Feelings can be expressed in many ways. The destructive way is in the form of violence. Unexpressed anger at ourselves becomes depression.

Dr. Valerie Hunt writes, "I know the longing for spiritual experience exists in all humans, for without it there is an unconscious sense that knowledge of the physical self and the material world is simply unsatisfying and insufficient. I accept the truism: When one represses emotion, the body hurts; when one represses consciousness, one's mind aches; when one represses spirituality, one's soul suffers."

Expressing Ourselves by Talking It Out

It is important to choose a safe person, one we can trust, to whom we reveal our deepest secrets, fears and resentments. We also need to choose wisely the person with whom we share our dreams so that they will not be laughed at or belittled. This person can be a minister or rabbi, friend or sponsor, counselor or therapist, teacher or parent. The important thing is that we feel safe enough to say whatever it is that we are holding on to, so as not to be haunted, consciously or subconsciously, by our unexpressed feelings.

The book *Alcoholics Anonymous* teaches its members to make a "strenuous effort to face, and to be rid of, the things in ourselves that have been blocking us . . . nothing counted but thoroughness and honesty."

EXPRESSING BY JOURNALING

Journal keeping requires courage and sweaters.
Courage because it's often hard and painful to see
your life before you in black and white;
sweaters because we all need
something to cozy up to.

—RICHARD SOLLY

Journaling is a very special and intimate time we take for ourselves. It can be used to record significant events or as a vehicle to help us through difficult times. It can help us become unstuck. Journaling can serve as a bridge, allowing us to leave our pain behind so that we can move past it. It is a safe container for our feelings.

I wrote pages and pages in my journal after my son died. I could not express my pain in any other way. My pain was so intense that I wrote what I was incapable of saying aloud. Some days the words just poured out; other days I just stared at the paper without any words at all, or I simply wrote a few words such as,

"Terrible day," or "Here I go again." My journal gave me great comfort and was a wonderful release. It became my friend.

To express how we feel, whether to another person or to the pages of our journal, helps us along the path of healing. Let the words and feelings come out. Don't be concerned about grammar or form. Your words don't even have to make sense. Let the pages be your safe container for your thoughts and feelings until you are ready to speak about them.

If you are concerned about other people reading your private thoughts, you can place a "Do Not Disturb Sign" on the door to the room where you keep your journal. Kathleen Adams, in her book *The Way of the Journal: A Journal Therapy Workbook for Healing*, suggests that we put on the front page of our journal: "Stop! This is the Personal Journal of: _____. Do Not Read Any Further Unless You Have Been Given Permission."

She also suggests the we write the word "breathe" at the top of every page and stop writing when we feel overwhelmed.

Expressing Ourselves by Letter Writing

Writing letters is another powerful tool for expressing and releasing painful, negative or destructive feelings. Perhaps you are very angry at someone who has hurt you. Express all your anger in a letter, writing everything you wouldn't say face to face. Get it all out. This is an exercise to become free in this moment. You might never send the letter at all, but write it anyway as if you are going to send it. Then put it away for at least twenty-four hours. At the end of that time you can decide to tone it down, send it as is or not send it at all.

Letter writing is especially useful if we want to release feelings to a person who has died. We might have amends to make and were not ready to make them while this person was alive. There might be things we never expressed, or perhaps we simply want to make a connection. Remember it is our intention here that counts. Whenever we are willing make our amends, we will be freed from our guilt.

What happened to John, a student in my meditation class, is a very good example of an appropriate action step.

John was very fond of his priest and was devastated when three young boys accused the priest of touching them inappropriately. John had been abused himself when he was young and had spent years working with a therapist to heal from his trauma. It had taken him a long time to rejoin his church and even longer to trust the new priest.

Without any hesitation, the church board decided to let the priest go. John was furious. He felt betrayed by both the priest and the board as well. What if the priest hadn't done anything wrong? The board hadn't even waited for an investigation.

All his old feelings were brought to the surface for John, and he was in very rough shape.

Finally, after weeks of being unable to eat or sleep well, John knew he had to take an action step, or he would soon be as sick as he was as a child. He attended the next board meeting and expressed his anger at the members for letting the priest go without a full investigation. The group listened politely to

John, and while they didn't reinstate the priest until they did investigate fully, they did apologize to him for their precipitous action.

John felt strong as he spoke. Something changed inside him. He was no longer a powerless little boy but a man of fairness and power. He then followed his heart and went to visit his friend, the priest, to see if he could be of comfort in any way.

It turned out that the boys had been upset with the priest for yelling at them when they had been late for choir practice. They wanted to get back at him and made up the story. The priest was invited back to the parish, but he knew he couldn't return. There would still be many members of the congregation who would always doubt him. He eventually received an invitation from another church who had heard of his circumstances and embraced him into their fold.

~

Another example of an action step is to simply change your thoughts. Recently, one of my clients was going through a difficult time looking for a new job. Each time a new job opened, something happened and it was no longer available. It was either changed to fewer hours, or the present employee decided not to leave after all. My client became more and more depressed, thinking everything was falling apart. As soon as she was able to switch her thinking to, "God is guiding me to the perfect job for me," her energy lifted and she was able to go out on a very positive interview that landed her a job beyond her expectations.

Visualizations

Visualizations, similar to changing our thoughts, are action steps we can take to bring changes to how we feel. They are excellent techniques to help us get in touch with our souls, to connect with our hearts and come from a place of love. Our bodies cannot discern the difference between real and imagined situations. Our bodies believe what our minds imagine, thereby responding to real or imagined situations in exactly the same way. For example, if we smell something burning and immediately think, *The building is on fire! I'm going to get hurt!* our bodies will believe this and immediately go into a flight mode. Adrenaline will be released and our breathing, pulse and heartbeat will become more rapid. On the other hand, if we smell something burning and think, *Something smells strange. I'd better check out what is going on,* we remain calm. Our bodies will remain relaxed because our thoughts remained calm. What we think becomes our reality.

Visualizations are excellent tools to turn our negative tapes into positive ones. They can help one begin to move away from fearful thoughts towards thoughts of love, peace, confidence and accomplishment. Athletes do this all the time by visualizing successful swings, putts, hoop shots, dives, etc. By imagining that you have already achieved new goals by creating a positive new picture in your mind, and then letting your body actually experience the feeling as if it has actually happened, you will be able to create new positive experiences with more and more ease.

Visualizations are like dress rehearsals. If you imagine a situation often enough, by the time that you actually find yourself in that situation, it will be familiar to you.

When we practice putting our hands over our hearts and imagining a time when we felt joy or love, or just a time when we felt good about ourselves, we are using visualizations in a very powerful way. Once we practice, we can retrieve our good feelings simply by putting our hands over our hearts.

Heart Memory Exercise

Imagine a time when you felt very confident or successful. Remember how that felt in your body. Now imagine something coming up that might cause you concern, such as a job interview or a confrontation with someone. Let yourself picture this situation. Let yourself feel what you felt when you were confident or successful. Practice this a few times before entering your new situation. If you do this often enough, new habits can be formed so that your mind and body will respond as you choose when you are in the actual situation.

Emmet Fox wrote that we provide the subconscious with the work to be done. He uses the example of an architect who prepares drawings of a completed house before the house has even been started. "He is drawing what is to be. So we build in thought the conditions that later come into manifestation on the physical plane."

Finding My Inner Sanctuary

You will reach down into your mind
to a new place of safety. You will recognize you have
reached it if you find a sense of deep peace ... how-
ever briefly. Let go of all trivial things that churn
and bubble on the surface of your mind, and reach
down below them. There is a place in you where
there is perfect peace.... There is a place in you
where nothing is impossible.... There is a
place in you where the strength of God,
Your Higher Power, lives.

—ADAPTED FROM *A Course in Miracles*

Creating a Special Place Inside

Here is a script you can read (or you can make up one of your
own). You can record this on tape if you wish, and then play it back
with your eyes closed; or read it in a relaxed, comfortable position.

There is a very special place inside each and every one of
us. It's a place where we feel perfectly safe, a place where we can
find peace. In your mind design a perfect place for yourself. It
can be anywhere, near the ocean or the mountains, the forest or
the desert—anywhere at all. It can be a place where you have
already been, or a brand new place in your imagination.

Create a place in your imagination where you feel absolutely safe and really good about yourself. This is your special place. No one else can go there unless you invite them. It's a place where you can be peaceful and relaxed.

Now be aware of your breath as it comes in and goes out.

Let yourself see your special place. Imagine you are walking to it now. Take some time to use all your senses to know your special place. Do you hear any special sounds? Smell any special aromas? How does the ground feel beneath your feet? What time of year is it? What time of day?

Imagine you have everything you need here . . . everything you want.

Create a place of comfort and relaxation.

Every time you breathe in, feel yourself filling with peace; as you breathe out, feel yourself releasing tension and anxiety. Feel peace flowing through your entire body. Spend some time feeling really good about yourself.

Know this is your special place, where you can always come to be alone, where you can find peace and inspiration.

Stay here as long as you wish and whenever you are ready, count to five before you open your eyes.

LETTING GO AFFIRMATION

*The fact that I can plant a seed and
it becomes a flower, share a bit of knowledge
and it becomes another's, smile at someone
and receive a smile in return, are to
me continual spiritual exercises.*

—LEO BUSCAGLIA

I know today that what I have been through can help someone else. The more I am willing to share my story, the more I am healing myself and helping someone else to heal. Just the fact that I have found the strength to come through something difficult can inspire courage and strength in another person.

Being open to share from my heart connects me with others and demonstrates that we are never alone. The comfort this can bring me far outweighs any desire I have for privacy and seclusion.

*God gives me all the courage I need to
be open and share from my heart, whenever my
story can help someone in need.*

CHAPTER 7

Joy and Purpose
. . . Forever

Eden

And then all that has divided us will merge

And then compassion will be wedded to power

And then softness will come to a world that is harsh and unkind

And then both men and women will be gentle

And then both women and men will be strong

And then no person will be subject to another's will

And then all will be rich and free and varied

And then the greed of some will give way to the needs of many

And then all will share equally in the earth's abundance

And then all will care for the sick and the weak and the old

And then all will nourish the young

And then all will cherish life's creatures

And then all will live in harmony with each other and the earth

And then everywhere will be called Eden once again.

—Merger poem by Judy Chicago

You are here to enable the divine purpose
of the universe to unfold. That is
how important you are!

—ECKHART TOLLE

L iving lightly is only one breath away. With willingness, the power of our intentions, practice and positive action, we can all live a life of joy and purpose. Our purpose changes as we change. When we are young, our purpose might be to be educated, to grow mentally, socially and spiritually. For some of us, our purpose might be just to survive, and this might last for many years. As we grow older, our purpose might be to be successful, to become good parents, to be financially responsible, proper citizens. Perhaps later, the care of our parents might be added to the list of our responsibilities.

In the midst of all this living, if we are growing spiritually, we are discovering who we are, what makes us tick and what our gifts are. Some of us may find we have special skills, and there is never a question about what we are supposed to do. Others struggle for years to discover their special gifts.

All of us long to feel connected, to belong to something greater than ourselves. All of us want to know why we are here on this earth. The power of our words and the energy of our thoughts offer us the incredible opportunity to belong to each other and find our highest purpose. Our energy can join with that of people all over the world who are meditating and praying for world peace.

In the steps of the Heart-Lightening Process, we have learned how to release all the blocks to joy, peace and love in our hearts. We are living lighter and lighter every day. As we become as light as a feather, our thought energy becomes more powerful, touching everyone around us. Rabbi Israel Salanter teaches, "First a person should put his house together, then his town, then the world."

Once you have mastered the simple techniques of the Heart-Lightening Process, you will discover that change occurs in three phases:

- You can experience an immediate lightening of your heart by learning to find peace in each moment.
- When you uncover your blocks to joy and learn how to eliminate their power over you, your heart will continually become more and more open.
- You will be connected to your soul forever and will intuitively know the next step on your spiritual path.

Critical Mass

When enough of us are aware of something,
all of us become aware of it.

—Ken Keyes Jr.

When a limited number of people know something in a new way, it remains the conscious property of only those people. But there is a point at which if only one more person tunes in to a new awareness, a field of energy is strengthened so that awareness of it is picked up by almost everyone, everywhere.[1]

Our peace can be contagious. As we become more peaceful, the lives of those around us can become more peaceful as well. As the energy around us becomes more peaceful, more people can feel it. As others take it in, they pass it on to people they meet, and so on, and so on.

I hope you pass on these simple techniques to others. Inspire them with your joyful spirit. Take time to make a commitment to inner and outer peace. Spend time in nature, with friends, with people and books that inspire you with positive energy. Spend time in prayer and meditation. Expand your generous spirit by doing something each day for someone else. Don't let a single negative thought destroy your peace of mind. Never forget gratitude, for gratitude is the antidote for self-pity, anger and resentments. Gratitude erases all blame and judgments, and leaves us with smiles and full hearts.

Remember, these are all goals. We are not looking for perfection but for progress. Our intention is what matters. We will still feel anger, greed, jealousy and the like. But we are learning not to act on our lower energy feelings. We feel them, accept them and choose to move on to higher, positive energy thoughts.

The Butterfly Effect

The chaos theory, discovered by meteorologist Edward Lorenze, demonstrated that a very small change in a system can have a profound effect. Tiny local actions can have widespread, far-off, complex consequences. The idea became known as the Butterfly Effect, after he gave a talk at the American Association for the Advancement of Science titled, "Predictability: Does the Flap of a Butterfly's Wings in Brazil Set Off a Tornado in Texas?"[2]

Ian Stewart, in his book *Does God Play Dice?* wrote, "The flapping of a single butterfly's wings today produces a tiny change in the state of the atmosphere. Over a period of time, the atmosphere actually diverges from what it would have done. So, in a month's time, a tornado that would have devastated the Indonesian coast doesn't happen. Or maybe one that wasn't going to happen, does."

We don't always know the results of our actions. But we do know that our actions produce results. For example, there have been many scientific experiments that prove that prayer does work. One study at the California Pacific Medical Center in San Francisco found that the AIDS patients who, without their knowledge, were prayed for had significantly fewer new AIDS-related diseases, less severe illness, fewer doctor visits, and fewer and shorter hospitalizations than patients in the control group who were not prayed for by those in the study.[3]

War can be but a memory. Let there be peace on earth and let it begin with me.

It is no longer acceptable that anyone suffers needlessly. As more and more of us continue to practice the Heart-Lightening Process—or any of the other numerous ways that help us live as light as a feather—and make meditation and prayer a regular part of our lives, many more people will be touched by our energies of joy, peace and love.

Metta is a wonderful Buddhist practice that helps us love ourselves and others and bring forgiveness to ourselves and to others. It is a powerful way to lighten our own hearts and help others to lighten theirs. The word "metta" is a Pali word with two root meanings. One is "gentle" and the other is "friend." We have to learn to love ourselves before we can bring love to anyone else. Once we can bring love to ourselves, then we can expand upon that love and send it to others. It becomes possible, if we are willing, to send love to someone who has harmed us so that we can release ourselves from our anger and resentments. Finally, we can send out this feeling of love to all people who are suffering.

Buddhist teacher and author Jack Kornfield tells us, "The quality of loving-kindness is the fertile soil out of which an integrated spiritual life can grow."

Begin by taking a few minutes to be with your breath, breathing in peace and breathing out tension. When you feel calm and relaxed, imagine that you are in your inner sanctuary. This is the place where your heart lives, a place where you feel love. Say to yourself:

May I be happy . . .
May I be peaceful . . .
May I be free from suffering.

Now bring someone into your heart who you care about and say:

May you be happy . . .
May you be peaceful . . .
May you be free from suffering.

Now, if you want to, bring in someone you would like to forgive or receive forgiveness from, or someone who you would like to see achieve peace, and say:

May you be joyful . . .
May you be peaceful . . .
May you be free from suffering.

Expand that feeling to everyone you know—your family, friends and colleagues—and say:

May you be joyful . . .
May you be peaceful . . .
May you be free from suffering.

And now extend that feeling to people with AIDS, cancer, and other life-threatening diseases, to the addicts and the alcoholics, the hungry and the homeless, the people at war, the people caught up in wars, and the people in power who think that war is the answer to peace, and say:

As we want to be joyful, may everyone be joyful . . .
As we want to be peaceful, may everyone be peaceful . . .
And as we want to be free from suffering, may everyone be free from suffering.
Peace.

The Heart-Lightening Process
Step 7:

LET GO AND LET GOD

No matter how well you are prepared,
the moment belongs to God.

—AUTHOR UNKNOWN

Once you have done your best to follow these steps, turn the results over to God, the universe or a higher power. Remember, our goal is to come from a place free from longing, accepting whatever is going on in the present moment. This is where joy lives. We are not in charge of the universe. God has a plan for us bigger than we can imagine.

One excellent exercise to help you let go is to use a God bag. Some people use God boxes. You can create a bag with your own design, making it as fancy as you wish, or simply use any paper or plastic bag you have on hand. Write the word "God" or "higher power" or "HP" on the bag—any word that makes you comfortable. Then write down all your fears, concerns and anxieties and put them in the bag.

You can also use your God bag for a decision you have to make or for a person or situation that is giving you a difficult time. Every time the feeling or thought comes up for you, know that you have placed it in the God bag. Know that you have turned it over. You don't have to worry about it any more. God or your higher power is handling it. There's nothing else you have to do about it. Answers will come to you at the appropriate time.

This is a powerful action step! First, there is our willingness to write about the disturbing situation at all, then there is the actual physical action of writing it. Both the willingness and the action are what make this step so successful.

By practicing the seven steps of the Heart-Lightening Process, you will find that you, too, will be living a much lighter life, full of joy and purpose.

LETTING GO AFFIRMATION

So watch the thought and its ways with care,
and let it spring from love, born
out of concern for all beings.

—BUDDHA

Whatever it is that I feel in my heart, I pass it on to others, knowingly or unknowningly. As I grow in my awareness of what is going on in my mind, I can direct my thoughts in the direction of my choice. This is so powerful! I can choose to feel peaceful and create an atmosphere of peace for myself and those around me. I can then send that feeling out into the universe, making a difference in the world.

Today I am taking time to fill my heart
with joy and love and compassion, sending them
out to everyone in the world with
a prayer for peace.

Endnotes

CHAPTER 1

1. *Larousse Encyclopedia of Mythology* (London: Batchworth Press Limitted, 1959), 41.

2. Time-Life Books, *Search for the Soul,* Mysteries of the Unknown (Alexandria, VA: Time-Life Books, 2000), 6–20, 139.

3. Rabbi David Cooper, *God Is a Verb* (New York: Riverhead Books, 1997), 78.

4. Rabbi Harold Kushner, *When Bad Things Happen to Good People* (New York: Avon Books, 1981), 71.

5. Maril Crabtree, *Sacred Feathers* (Avon, MA: Adams Media Corporation, 2002), xii.

6. Ruth Fishel, *Time for Joy* (Deerfield Beach, FL: Health Communications, Inc., 1988), 1.

CHAPTER 2

1. Marion Woodward, "Worshiping Illusions," *Parabola* 12:2 (May 1987) 64.

2. Ruth Fishel, *Stop! Do You Know You're Breathing?*

Simple Techniques for Teachers and Parents to Reduce Stress and Violence in the Classroom and at Home (Marstons Mills, MA: Spirithaven, 2000).

3. Tape by meditation teacher and author Jack Kornfield.

4. Definition of Insight Meditation from the Insight Meditation Society brochure in Barrie, MA. Reprinted with permission.

CHAPTER 3

1. Gail Goodwin, *Heart* (New York: Harper-Collins Publishers, 2001).

2. Doc Childre and Howard Martin with Donna Beech, *The Heartmath Solution* (New York: HarperCollins Publishers, 1999), 4–5.

3. Ibid., 28–29.

4. Paul Pearsall, *The Heart's Code* (New York: Broadway Books, 1998), 4–5.

5. Ibid., 59.

6. Ibid., 7.

7. Goodwin, *Heart,* 34–35.

8. Ibid., 44.

9. Childre, Martin and Beech, *The Heartmath Solution,* x.

10. Wayne Dyer, *There's a Spiritual Solution to Every Problem,* (New York: HarperCollins, 2001) 44; referring

to Dr. Valerie Hunt, *Infinite Mind* (Malibu, CA: Malibu Publishing, 1989, 1995, 1996).

11. David R. Hawkins, *Power vs. Force* (Carlsbad, CA: Hay House, Inc., 1995, 1998, 2002), 68–69.

12. Hawkins, *Power vs. Force.*

13. Hawkins, *Power vs. Force,* 75–100, 106.

14. Childre, Martin and Beech, *Heartmath Solution,* 69.

CHAPTER 4

1. Bill Wilson, *As Bill Sees It: The A.A. Way of Life . . . Selected Writings of A.A.'s Co-Founder* (New York: Alcohol Anonymous World Service, 1999), 263.

2. Ibid., 196.

3. Childre, Martin and Beech, *The Heartmath Solution,* 63.

4. Charlotte Joko Beck, *Nothing Special* (San Francisco: Harper, 1994), 105.

5. Dalai Lama and Howard C. Cutler, *The Art of Happiness* (Mew York: Riverhead Books, 1998), 293.

6. Ruth Fishel, *Change Almost Anything in 21 Days* (Deerfield Beach, FL: Health Communications, Inc., 2003).

CHAPTER 5

1. Rabbi Gary Mazo, *And the Flames Did Not Consume Us* (Scotts Valley, CA: Rising Star Press, 2000), 98.

CHAPTER 6

1. Alcoholic Anonymous World Service, *AA Comes of Age* (New York: Alcoholics Anonymous Publishing, now known as World Services, Inc.) 63.

CHAPTER 7

1. Ruth Fishel, *Precious Solitude* (Holbrook, MA: Adams Media Corporation, 1999) and *Change Almost Anything in 21 Days* (Deerfield Beach, FL: Health Communications, Inc., 2003).

2. Sharon Salzberg, *Faith* (New York: Riverhead Books, 2002), 138–139.

3. Ibid., 144.

About the Author

R uth Fishel, M.Ed., is a prolific author, national retreat and workshop leader and meditation teacher. She is co-founder of SpiritHaven of Cape Cod. Her books include: the bestselling *Change Almost Anything in 21 Days, Time for Joy, The Journey Within, Hang In 'Til the Miracle Happens, Stop! Do You Know You're Breathing?* and *Precious Solitude.*

Ruth has also created SpiritLifters, a line of inspirational greeting cards. Her classes, books and workshops take you on a marvelous journey through pain and loss to inspiration and hope. They provide you with a gentle path to growth, peace and love.

She can be reached at *spirithaven@spirithaven.com* or through her Web site at *www.spirithaven.com* or phone (508) 420-5301.

BOOK AND TAPES
by Ruth Fishel

Change Almost Anything in 21 Days

Hang In 'Til the Miracle Happens

Precious Solitude

Stop! Do You Know You're Breathing?

Simple Techniques for Teachers and Parents to
    Reduce Stress and Violence in the Classroom
    and at Home

The Journey Within: A Spiritual Path to Recovery

Time for Joy: Daily Meditation and Affirmations
    Which has sold over 300,000 copies

Take Time for Yourself!

Cape Cod Memories

Newport Memories

Memories of the Florida Coast

AUDIOTAPES

Time for Joy

You Can't Meditate Wrong

**Transforming Your Past Into Presents: Guided
    Exercises for Deepening Your Meditation
    Experience**

**The Journey Within: Discovering Your Source
    of Peace**

For more information about Ruth's workshops, retreats, books, tapes and greeting cards, write to *spirit haven@spirithaven.com*, go to her Web site *www. spirithaven.com* or call her at (508) 420-5301.

More from Ruth Fishel

Time for Thoughtfulness
A Daily Guide to Filling the World with Love, Care and Compassion

By Ruth Fishel
Illustrations by Bonny Van de Kamp

Code #3227 • Paperback • $7.95

Travel through a calender year with inspiring quotes, uplifting thoughts and heartwarming affirmations.

Heal your wounded spirit with this beautiful collection of uplifting affirmations.

By the Bestselling Author of *Time for Joy*

TAKE TIME FOR YOURSELF

RUTH FISHEL

MEDITATIVE MOMENTS FOR HEALTHY LIVING

Illustrations by Bonny Van de Kamp

Code #6855 • Paperback • $8.95

Also from Ruth Fishel

Code #4419 • Paperback • $8.95

**Let this beautifully written book transport you
to the place where healing begins.**